Build It Now

Build It Now:
Socialism for the Twenty-First Century

Michael A. Lebowitz

MONTHLY REVIEW PRESS
New York

Library of Congress Cataloging-in-Publication Data

Lebowitz, Michael A.
   Build it now : socialism for the twenty-first century / Michael A. Lebowitz.
      p. cm.
         Includes bibliographical references and index.
         ISBN 1-58367-145-5 (pbk. : alk. paper) — ISBN 1-58367-146-3
         (cloth : alk. paper)

1. Socialism.   I. Title.
   HX73.L416 2006
   335—dc22
         2006011445

   Designed by Terry J. Allen

   Monthly Review Press
   122 West 27th Street
   New York, NY 10001
   www.monthlyreview.org

   10 9 8 7 6 5 4 3 2 1

   Printed in Canada

For Marta, who looks in the same direction.

Contents

Introduction

The nature of capitalism, Marx once noted, comes to the surface in a crisis. Then, it is possible to see some things that were hidden—that the whole system revolves around profits and not human needs. Yet, we see every day what capitalism produces. The blatant waste in advertising, the destruction of the planet, the starvation of children alongside the obscene salaries of professional athletes, the despotic workplace and the treatment of human beings as so much garbage, the coexistence of unused resources, unemployed people, and people with unmet needs—these are not accidents in the world of capitalism. Things could not be otherwise, Marx commented, where workers exist for the growth of capital—as opposed to the "inverse situation" in which the results of social labor are there "to satisfy the worker's own need for development."

In the twentieth century, an alternative to capitalism emerged. It involved different relations of production—society was not driven by the profit motive. Nor was there the inverse situation, in which the worker's need for self-development dominates. Rather, characteristic of the new form was the use of the state to develop productive forces as rapidly as possible. Certainly one element shaping this alternative was the belief that it was necessary to catch up to capitalism in order to avoid military defeat. (We must make up the gap within ten years, Stalin stated in 1931, or we will be defeated.) But, there was also, with some exceptions, the general conception that all history depends on the expansion of the productive forces (which, in practice, meant the means of production), leaving little room for exploration of the relevance of the social relations in which people live.

There have been continuing debates over what this twentieth-century alternative was. Socialism, state socialism, state capitalism, statism, bureaucratic centralism, bureaucratically deformed workers' state or—my own proposal—vanguard mode of production? Isn't it time, though, to move away from the imperative of choosing among these (which means choosing among various sects that have differentiated their products) and simply recognize that what emerged in the last century was definitely not the concept of socialism that Marx envisioned?

Of course, we need to acknowledge that the products of the last century were and are flawed. But not so we can demonstrate our superior abstract wisdom by offering "critical support" to these flawed efforts (which in most cases has all the relevance of offering critical support to feudalism in the struggle against slavery) but, rather, so we can learn and carry on our struggle to build a better world.

The title of this book comes from the slogan of the South African Communist Party: "Socialism is the future, build it now." Regardless of the practice of the SACP, I've always felt that the slogan is profound—precisely because that slogan simultaneously recognizes the need for a vision that can guide us, indicating where we want to go, and also stresses the need for activity, the need to struggle for that goal now. This combination of vision and struggle is essential. In the struggle to realize the vision of a new society, we not only change the old society, we also change ourselves, and, as Marx commented, make ourselves fit to create the new society.

Although the essays in this book come from various sources, most relate in some way to Venezuela, a country which at the time of writing embodies the hopes of many for a real alternative to capitalism. For example, chapter 2, "Ideology and Economic Development," originates both from my understanding of mainstream economics from years of teaching and also from my experience with Canada's social democratic party, the New Democratic Party (including the period when I was provincial policy chair during the 1972–75 government in British Columbia). While these two sources yield rather dreary perspectives, the apparent optimism in the paper (presented at the annual conference on Globalization and Problems of Development in Havana in February 2004) reflected my growing recognition of what was beginning in Venezuela.

"The Knowledge of a Better World," chapter 3, presented at the meeting of Artists and Intellectuals in Defense of Humanity in Caracas in December 2004, presents two perspectives on knowledge—knowledge as commodity in the world of capital and knowledge in a better world, one that corresponds to the vision of Marx. As in the preceding paper, the focus here is upon the importance of a vision, one stressing the centrality of human development. This point is explicit in the fourth chapter, "Reclaiming a Socialist Vision," based upon an earlier talk in the context of working within an anti-capitalist coalition, Rebuilding the Left. In it I argue the necessity to go beyond anti-capitalism to a concept of socialism.

The remaining three chapters directly reflect the Venezuelan experience, which I have been privileged to observe closely over the last few years (functioning as an advisor in the Ministry for the Social Economy in 2004). In the context of the growing discussions of a socialist path for Venezuela, chapter 5, "Socialism Doesn't Drop from the Sky," was presented to a national gathering of students assembled in July 2005 for the purpose of exploring socialism for the twenty-first century. Drawing upon my work on both Marx and on the experience of efforts in the twentieth century, this essay offers an approach to conceiving what socialism is—and what it is not—consistent with the vision embodied in the Bolivarian constitution.

Among other things, that constitution stresses the importance of worker management, self-management, and co-management for the development of human potential. In the April 2004 Solidarity meeting in Caracas, I introduced the lessons of Yugoslav self-management. Within the coming year, the experiences of worker management multiplying, I returned to the subject at the 2005 Solidarity meetings—this time stressing the *problems* in self-management (especially the self-orientation of workers and the separation of workers and community) that had to be resolved. This is the subject of chapter 6, "Seven Difficult Questions."

The final chapter, "The Revolution of Radical Needs," was written specifically for this volume. Here, as with my other essays and talks related to Venezuela, I have benefited much from continuing discussions with my partner, Marta Harnecker. While still working on this chapter, however, another person with whom I regularly shared my thoughts and information about Venezuela died. I feel a deep loss (as do so many) with the death of Harry Magdoff—especially because I would have liked to have shared this chapter with him (as I had all the others). At ninety-two, Harry was very enthusiastic about what was happening in Venezuela and, characteristically, indicated that if he were only eighty years old again, he would be there.

In one of his last works, "Approaching Socialism" (*Monthly Review*, July–August 2005), Harry, writing with his son Fred Magdoff, stressed that the evils of capitalism flow out of its very nature. "A new society," they wrote, "is needed because the evils are part of the DNA of the capitalist system." Precisely because the critical social, economic, and environmental problems of the world are inherent in that system, "capitalism must be replaced with an economy and society at the service of humanity—necessitating also the creation of an environment that protects the earth's life-support systems."

This is the starting point for *Build It Now* as well. We need to understand the genetic program of capitalism, how the horrors we see around us are not accidents but inherent in the system—that they are not the result of particularly bad caretakers of capitalism, accordingly calling for their replacement by good caretakers. *Build It Now* begins by attempting to understand the DNA of capitalism. Chapter 1, "The Needs of Capital versus the Needs of Human Beings," written originally for a collection of essays on capitalism, stresses the way in which the logic of capital is contrary to the need for human development. In doing so, it points to the need to go beyond capitalism to a world fit for the human family. The choice before us is socialism or barbarism. Which one shall it be?

Caracas, Venezuela
February 2006

1

The Needs of Capital versus
the Needs of Human Beings

Like other early nineteenth-century socialists, Karl Marx's vision of the good society was one that would unleash the full development of all human potential.[1] "What is the aim of the Communists?" asked Marx's comrade Friedrich Engels in his early draft of the *Communist Manifesto*. "To organize society in such a way that every member of it can develop and use all his capabilities and powers in complete freedom and without thereby infringing the basic conditions of this society." In Marx's final version of the *Manifesto*, that new society appears as an "association, in which the free development of each is the condition for the free development of all."[2]

This idea of the development of human potential runs throughout Marx's work—the possibility of rich human beings with rich human needs, the potential for producing human beings as rich as possible in needs and capabilities. What indeed is wealth, he asked, "other than the universality of individual needs, capacities, pleasures, productive forces?" Think about the "development of the rich individuality which is as all-sided in its production as in its consumption"; think about "the absolute working out of his creative potentialities." The real goal is the "development of all human powers as such the end in itself."

Realization of this potential, however, cannot drop from the sky. It requires the development of a society in which people do not look upon each other as separate, one where we consciously recognize our interdependence and freely cooperate upon the basis of that recognition. When we relate to each other as human beings, Marx proposed, we produce for each other simply because we understand that others need the results of our activity, and we get pleasure and satisfaction from the knowledge that we are accomplishing something worthwhile. Your need would be sufficient to ensure my activity, and, in responding, I would be "confirmed both in your thought and your love." What Marx was describing, of course, is the concept of a human family.

Marx's vision of a society of freely associated producers, a profoundly moral and ethical one, led him quite early in his life to pose certain analytical questions. What is it about this society in which we now live that if you were to tell me you had a need for something I was capable of satisfying, it would be considered as a plea, a humiliation, "and consequently uttered with a feeling of shame, of degradation"? Why is it, he asked, that rather than affirming that I am capable of activity that helps another human being, your needs are instead a source of power for me? "Far from being the *means* which would give you *power* over my production, they [your needs] are instead the *means* for giving me power over you."

As long as we relate to one another not as members of a human community but as self-seeking owners, Marx concluded, this perverted separation of people is constantly reproduced. So, Marx was led to explore the nature of the social relations that exist between people, the character of the relations in which they engage in producing—producing for themselves as well as producing for each other. It was how he proceeded to analyze capitalism.

Capitalist Relations of Production

The story told by economists who celebrate capitalism is that competition and markets ensure that capitalists will satisfy the needs of people—not because of their humanity and benevolence but, as Adam Smith put it, "from a regard to their own interest." Competing on the market with other capitalists, they are driven (as if whipped by an invisible hand) to serve the people. For Marx, though, this focus upon competition and markets obscures exactly what distinguishes capitalism from other market economies—its specific relations of production. There are two central aspects of capitalist relations of production—the side of capitalists and the side of workers. On the one hand, there are capitalists—the owners of wealth, the owners of the physical and material means of production. And their orientation is toward the growth of their wealth. Beginning with capital of a certain value in the form of money, capitalists purchase commodities with the goal of gaining *more* money, additional value, surplus value. And that's the point, profits. As capitalists, all that matters for them is the growth of their capital.

On the other hand, we have workers—people who have neither material goods they can sell nor the material means of producing the things they need for themselves. Without those means of production, they can't produce commodities to sell in the market to exchange. So, how do they get the things they need? By selling the only thing they have to sell, their ability to work. They can sell it to whomever they choose, but they cannot choose *whether or not* to sell their power to perform labor (if they are to survive).

Before we can talk about capitalism, in short, certain conditions must already be present. Not only must there be a commodity-money economy in which some people are the owners of means of production but also there must be a special commodity available on the market—the capacity to perform labor. For that to happen, Marx proposed, workers first must be free in a double sense. They must be free to sell their labor-power (i.e., have property rights in their capacity to perform labor—something the slave, e.g., lacks) and they must be "free" of means of production (i.e., the means of production must have been separated from producers). In other words, one aspect unique to capitalist relations of production is that it is characterized by the existence of people who, lacking the means of production, are able and compelled to sell a property right, the right of disposition over their ability to work. They are compelled to sell their power to produce in order to get money to buy the things they need.

Yet it is important to understand that while the separation of the means of production from producers is a necessary condition for capitalist relations of production, it is not a sufficient condition. If workers are separated from the means of production, there remain two possibilities: (1) workers sell their labor-power to the owners of means of production; or (2) workers rent means of production from their owners. There is a long tradition in mainstream economics that proposes it doesn't matter whether capital hires labor or labor hires capital because the results will be the same in both cases. For Marx, as we will see, there was a profound difference: only the first case, where capital has taken possession of production and the sale of labor-power occurs, is capitalism; only there do we see the unique characteristics of capitalism.

But it is not simply wage-labor that is critical. Capitalism requires both the existence of labor-power as a commodity and its combination with *capital*. Who buys that particular property right in the market and why? The capitalist buys the right to dispose of the worker's capacity to perform labor precisely because it is a means to achieve *his* goal, profits. Because that and only that, the growth of his capital, is what interests him as a capitalist.

Well, we now have the basis for an exchange between two parties in the market, the owner of money and the owner of labor-power. Each wants what the other has; each gets something out of that exchange. It looks like a free transaction. This is the point at which most non-Marxist economics stops. It looks at the transactions that take place in the market, and it declares, "we see freedom." This is what Marx described as "the realm of Freedom, Equality, Property, and Bentham." In fact, since the "free-trader *vulgaris*" sees *only* the transactions in the marketplace, he sees only freedom.

But this is not *every* market economy we are describing here. Not every market economy is characterized by the sale of labor-power to a capitalist. A defense of a market economy as such is not a defense of capitalism—no more than a defense of the market is a defense of slavery (which of course involves the buying and selling of slaves). This distinction between capitalism and markets, though, is not one the defenders of capitalism tend to make—their ideology, Marx proposed, leads them to confuse on principle the characteristics of pre-capitalist market economies with capitalism.

Why? Think about what is unique about this market economy in which labor-power has been sold to the capitalist. Now that the market transaction is over, Marx commented, we see that something has happened to each of the two parties. "He who was previously the money-owner now strides out in front as a capitalist; the possessor of labor-power follows as his worker." And where are they going? They are entering the place of work; they are entering the place where the capitalist now has the opportunity to *use* that property right he has purchased.

The Sphere of Capitalist Production

Two central characteristics exist in the process of production that takes place under capitalist relations. First, the worker works under the direction, supervision, and control of the capitalist. The goals of the capitalist determine the nature and purpose of production. Directions and orders in the production process come to workers from above. There is no horizontal relationship between capitalist and worker as buyer and seller in the marketplace here; there is no market here. Rather, there is a vertical relation between the one who has power and the one who does not. It is a command system, what Marx described as the despotism of the capitalist workplace. So much for the realm of freedom and equality.

And *why* does the capitalist have this power over workers here? Because he purchased the right to dispose of their ability to perform labor. That was the property right he purchased. It was the property right that the worker sold and *had* to sell because it was the only option available if she were to survive.

The second characteristic of capitalist production is that workers have no property rights in the product that results from their activity. They have no claim. They have sold to the capitalist the only thing that might have given them a claim, the capacity to perform labor. In contrast to producers in a cooperative who benefit from their own efforts because they have property rights in the products they produce, when workers work harder or more productively in the capitalist firm, they increase the value of the *capitalist's* property. Unlike a cooperative (which is not characterized by capitalist relations of production), in the capitalist firm all the fruits of the worker's productive activity belong to the capitalist, the residual claimant. This is why the sale of labor-power is so critical as a distinguishing characteristic of capitalism.

What happens, then, in the sphere of capitalist production? It all follows logically from the nature of capitalist relations of production. Insofar as the capitalist's goal is surplus value, he only purchases labor-power to the extent that it will generate that surplus value. For Marx, the necessary condition for generation of surplus value was the performance of surplus labor—the performance of labor over and above the labor contained in what the capitalist pays as wages. The capitalist, through the combination of his control of production and ownership of the product of labor, will act to ensure that workers add more value in production than the capitalist has paid them.

How does this occur? At any given point, we can calculate the hours of daily labor that are necessary to maintain workers at their existing standard of living. Those hours of "necessary labor," Marx proposed, are determined by the relationship between the existing standard of necessity (the real wage) and the general level of productivity. If productivity rises, then less hours of labor would be necessary for workers to reproduce themselves. Simple. Of course, the capitalist has no interest in a situation in which workers work only long enough to maintain themselves. What the capitalist wants is workers to perform *surplus* labor—i.e., that the labor performed by workers (the capitalist workday) *exceeds* the level of necessary labor. The ratio between surplus labor and necessary labor, Marx defined as the rate of exploitation (or, in its monetary form, the rate of surplus value).

We now have in place the elements that can illustrate what Marx referred to as the "law of motion," i.e., the dynamic properties, which flow from these particular capitalist relations of production. Remember that the whole purpose of the process from the point of view of the capitalist is profits. The worker is only a means to this end—the growth of capital. Let us begin with an extreme assumption—that the workday is equal to the level of necessary labor (i.e., there is no surplus labor). If this case were to remain true, there would be no capitalist production. So, what can the capitalist do in order to achieve his goal?

One option for the capitalist is to use his control over production to increase the work that the laborer performs. Extend the workday, make the workday as long as possible. A 10-hour workday? Fine. A 12-hour workday? Better. The worker will perform more work for the capitalist over and above the wage, and capital will grow. Another way is by intensifying the workday. Speed-up. Make workers work harder and faster in a given time period. Make sure there is no wasted motion, no slack time. Every moment workers rest is time they are not working for capital.

Another option for the capitalist is to reduce what he pays. Drive down the real wage. Bring in people who will work for less. Encourage people to compete with each other to see who will work for the least. Bring in immigrants, impoverished people from the countryside. Relocate to where you can get cheap labor.

That is the inherent logic of capital. The inherent tendency of capital is to increase the exploitation of workers. In the one case, the workday is increasing; in the other, the real wage is falling. In both cases, the rate of exploitation is driven upward. Marx commented that "the capitalist [is] constantly tending to reduce wages to their physical minimum and extend the working day to its physical maximum." He continued, however, saying, "while the working man constantly presses in the opposite direction."

In other words, within the framework of capitalist relations, while capital pushes to increase the workday both in length and intensity and to drive down wages, workers struggle to reduce the workday and to increase wages. They form trade unions for this purpose. Just as there is struggle from the side of capital, so also is there class struggle from the side of the worker. Why? Take the struggle over the workday, for example. Why do the workers want more time for themselves? Marx refers to "time for education, for intellectual development, for the fulfillment of social functions, for social intercourse, for the free play of the vital forces of his body and his mind." Time, Marx noted, is "the room of human development. A man who has no free time to dispose of, whose whole lifetime, apart from the mere physical interruptions by sleep, meals, and so forth, is absorbed by his labor for the capitalist, is less than a beast of burden."

What about the struggle for higher wages? Of course, there are the physical requirements to survive that must be obtained. But Marx understood that workers necessarily need much more than this. The worker's social needs include "the worker's participation in the higher, even cultural satisfactions, the agitation for his own interests, newspaper subscriptions, attending lectures, educating his children, developing his taste, etc." In short, workers have their own goals. As they are beings within society, their needs are necessarily socially determined. Their needs as human beings within society stand opposite capital's own inherent tendencies in production. When we look at the side of the worker, we recognize, as Marx did, "the worker's own need for development."

From the perspective of capital, though, workers and, indeed, all human beings, are only means. They are not an end. And if satisfying the goals of capital require employing racism, dividing workers, using the state to outlaw or destroy unions, destroying the lives and futures of people by shutting down operations and moving to parts of the world where people are poor and unions are banned, so be it. Capitalism has never been a system whose priority is human beings and their needs.

True, wages have increased and the workday has been reduced since Marx wrote. But that doesn't invalidate Marx's description of capitalism—every gain occurs despite the opposition of capitalists (as it did in Marx's time). Writing about the Ten-Hours Bill, the law that reduced the length of the workday in England to ten hours, Marx described it as a great victory, a victory over "the blind rule of the supply and demand laws" that form the political economy of the capitalist class; it was the first time, he noted, that "in broad daylight the political economy of the [capitalist] class succumbed to the political economy of the working class."

In other words, the gains that workers make are the result of their struggles. They press in the opposite direction to capital; they struggle to reduce the rate of exploitation. And, implicit in that political economy of workers and in the struggles of working people is the overcoming of divisions among them (whatever their source). None of this is new. Marx described the hostility at the time between English and Irish workers as the source of their weakness: "It is the secret by which the capitalist class maintains its power. And that class is fully aware of it." In this respect, the struggle between capitalists and workers is a struggle over the degree of separation among workers.

Precisely because workers (given their needs as human beings) do resist reduced wages and increased workdays, capitalists must find a different way for capital to grow; they are forced to introduce machinery in order to increase productivity. By increasing productivity relative to the real wage, they lower necessary labor and increase the rate of exploitation. In the struggle between capital and labor, Marx argued, capitalists are driven to revolutionize the production process.

Marx traced in *Capital* the manner in which capitalists historically altered the mode of production in order to achieve their goals. Beginning with the preexisting mode of production (one characterized by small-scale craftwork), capitalists used their control over production, their ability to subordinate workers, to extend and intensify the workday. There are, however, inherent barriers to this method of expanding surplus value and capital, barriers given by both the physiological limits to the workday and the resistance of workers. Accordingly, capitalists proceeded to introduce new divisions of labor, new forms of social cooperation under their control, in an altered production process. An important effect was to increase productivity and foster the growth of capital.

Yet, even within this new form of manufacturing characterized by new divisions of labor within the workplace, there remained barriers to the growth of capital. This form of production remained dependent upon skilled workers, with their long periods of apprenticeship, and was subject to the resistance of those skilled workers to the rule of capital within the workplace. Marx detailed, then, how capital proceeded by the mid-nineteenth century to go beyond these barriers to its growth by altering the mode of production further—it introduced machinery and the factory system. With this development of what Marx called "the specifically capitalist mode of production," capital subordinates workers not merely by its power to command within the workplace but by their real domination by capital in the form of machines. Rather than workers employing means of production, means of production employ workers.

Tracing the logic of capital well beyond the alterations in the mode of production that had occurred in his own lifetime, Marx described the emergence of large automated factories, organic combinations of machinery that perform all the intricate operations of production. In these "organs of the human brain, created by the human hand," all scientific knowledge and the products of the social brain appear as attributes of capital rather than of the collective workers; and the workers employed within these "automatic factories" themselves appear as insignificant, stepping "to the side of the production process instead of being its chief actor."

The transformation of production through the incorporation of the products of the social brain not surprisingly generates the potential for enormous productivity increases. A good thing, obviously—it has the potential to eliminate poverty in the world, to make possible a substantially reduced workday (one that can provide time for human development). Yet, remember those are not the goals of the capitalist, and that is not why capital introduces these changes in the mode of production. Rather than a reduced workday, what capital wants is reduced necessary labor; what it wants is to maximize surplus labor and the rate of exploitation.

Similarly, because it is not increased productivity but only increased profits that motivate capitalists, the particular technology and technique of production selected is not necessarily the most efficient; rather, given that workers have their own goals, the logic of capital points to the selection of techniques that will divide workers from one another and permit easier surveillance and monitoring of their performance. It is, of course, no concern of capital whether the technology chosen permits producers to find any pleasure and satisfaction in their work. Nor is it a concern what happens to people who are displaced when new technology and new machines are introduced. If your skills are destroyed, if your job disappears, so be it. Capital gains, you lose. Marx's comment was that "within the capitalist system all methods for raising the social productivity of labor are put into effect at the cost of the individual worker."

There is another important aspect to the introduction of machinery. Every worker displaced by the substitution of machinery adds to what Marx described as the reserve army of labor. Not only does the existence of this body of unemployed workers permit capital to exert discipline within the workplace, but it also keeps wages within limits consistent with profitable capitalist production. The constant replenishing of the reserve army ensures that even those workers who, by organizing and struggle, may "achieve a certain quantitative participation in the general growth of wealth," nevertheless would not succeed in keeping real wages rising as rapidly as productivity. The rate of exploitation, Marx believed, would continue to rise. Even with rising real wages, the "abyss between the life situation of the worker and that of the capitalist would keep widening."

In short, Marx offers a picture in which capital has the upper hand in the sphere of production. Through its control of production and over the nature and direction of investment, it can increase the degree of exploitation of workers and expand the production of surplus value. While it may face opposition from workers, capital drives beyond barriers to its growth in the sphere of production. But Marx noted that there was an inherent contradiction in capitalism in this respect: capital cannot remain in the sphere of production but must return to the sphere of circulation and there sell its products as commodities—not in some abstract market but in one marked by the specific conditions of capitalist production.

The Sales Effort and "Overproduction"

Insofar as capital succeeds in the sphere of production, it produces more and more commodities containing surplus value. However, capitalists do not want these commodities. What they want is to *sell* those commodities and to make real the surplus value latent within them; i.e., they must reenter the sphere of circulation (this time as sellers) to realize their potential profits. And here, Marx noted, they face a new barrier to their growth—the extent of the market. Accordingly, capitalists turn their attention to finding ways to transcend that barrier—just as they are driven to increase surplus value within the sphere of production, so also are they driven to increase the size of the market in order to realize that surplus value. Thus, Marx talked about how "just as capital has the tendency on the one side to create ever more surplus labor, so it has the complementary tendency to create more points of exchange." Whatever the size of market, capitalists are always attempting to expand it. Marx noted, indeed, that "the tendency to create the world market is directly given in the concept of capital itself. Every limit appears as a barrier to be overcome."

How, then, does capital expand the market? By propagating existing needs in a wider circle, by "the production of *new* needs"—the *sales effort*.[3] Once you understand the nature of capitalism, you can see why capital is necessarily driven to expand the sphere of circulation; it was only in the twentieth century that the spread and development of the "specifically capitalist mode of production" made the sales effort so overwhelming. The enormous expenditures in modern capitalism upon advertising, the astronomical salaries offered to professional athletes whose presence can increase viewership and thereby the advertising revenues that may be captured by media outlets—what else is this (and so much like it) but testimony to capital's successes in the sphere of production and its compulsion to succeed similarly in *selling* the commodities produced? For those commodities latently containing surplus value to make the "mortal leap" of sale successfully, capital must invest heavily in the sphere of circulation (which in a rational society would be grasped as an unacceptable waste of human and material resources).

Capital's problem in the sphere of circulation, though, is not simply that it must expand the sphere of circulation, it is that capital tends to expand the production of surplus value *beyond* its ability to realize that surplus value. Overproduction, Marx indicated, is "the fundamental contradiction of developed capital." There is a constant tendency toward overproduction of capital, a tendency to expand productive capacity more than the existing capitalist market will justify. Capitalist production takes place "without any consideration for the actual limits of the market or the needs backed by the ability to pay." Accordingly, there exists a "constant tension between the restricted dimensions of consumption on the capitalist basis, and a production that is constantly striving to overcome these immanent barriers."

For Marx, this inherent tendency of capital to produce more surplus value than it can realize flows directly from capital's successes in the sphere of production—in particular, its success in driving up the rate of exploitation. What capital does in the sphere of production comes back to haunt it in the sphere of circulation: by striving "to reduce the relation of this necessary labor to surplus labor to the minimum," capital simultaneously creates "barriers to the sphere of exchange, i.e., the possibility of realization—the realization of the value posited in the production process." Overproduction, Marx commented, arises precisely because the consumption of workers "does not grow correspondingly with the productivity of labor."

A period of great increases in productivity while real wages lag behind—this is a recipe for overaccumulation of capital and its effects (as occurred in the Great Depression of the 1930s). How far are we from that now, with an enormous growth in productive capacity around the world in countries with low wages and a constant replenishing of the reserve army as peasants move (or are driven) from the countryside? The ability of capital to move to low-wage countries to manufacture commodities that are exported back to the more developed world significantly increases the gap between productivity and real wages—it increases the rate of exploitation in the world. And it means that the sales effort to move commodities through the sphere of circulation must intensify. In this respect, there is more than just an obscene contrast between the low wages of women producing Nike shoes and the high endorsement fees of the Michael Jordans; there is, indeed, an organic link.

The first sign of overaccumulation of capital is intensified competition among capitalists. (Why would that happen if the ability to produce surplus value were *not* outrunning the growth of the market?) However, the ultimate effect of overproduction is crisis, those "momentary, violent solutions for the existing contradictions, violent eruptions that reestablish the disturbed balance for the time being." Inventories of unsold commodities grow. But if commodities cannot be sold under existing market conditions, they will not be produced under capitalism. And so, production is reduced, layoffs are announced—even though the potential to produce is there and people's needs are there. Capitalism is not, after all, in the business of charity.

In the crisis, the nature of capitalism is there for everyone to see: *profits —rather than the needs of people as socially developed human beings—determine the nature and extent of production within capitalism.* What other economic system can you imagine that could generate the simultaneous existence of unused resources, unemployed people, and people with unmet needs for what could be produced? What other economic system would allow people to starve in one part of the world while elsewhere there is an abundance of food and where the complaint is "too much food is being produced"?

The Reproduction of Capital

There's so much more to say about Marx's analysis of capitalism—far more than any short introduction could hope to present. The increasing concentration of capital in the hands of a few large corporations, the division of the world into haves and have-nots, the use of the state by capital—all this can be found in Marx's examination of capitalism. So, too, a profound grasp of the incompatibility between the logic of capital and Nature, between "the entire spirit of capitalist production, which is oriented toward the most immediate monetary profit" and the "permanent conditions of life required by the chain of human generations." Capitalist production, he commented, develops the social process of production "by simultaneously undermining the original sources of all wealth—the soil and the worker."[4]

Enough has been said to grasp the essential story of capitalism that Marx painted, one in which the needs of capital stand opposite the needs of human beings. It is a picture of an expanding system that both tries to deny human beings the satisfaction of their needs and also constantly conjures up new, artificial needs to induce them to purchase commodities—a Leviathan that devours the working lives of human beings and Nature in pursuit of profits, that destroys the skills of people overnight, and that in the name of progress thwarts the worker's own need for development. So, why is this abomination still around?

It would be a big mistake to think that Marx believed that replacing capitalism would be an easy matter. True, capitalism was subject to periodic crises, but Marx was clear that these crises weren't permanent. He never thought that someday capitalism would just collapse. Nevertheless, the nature of the system comes to the surface in a crisis. Furthermore, it becomes more transparent with the growing concentration of capital. So, isn't that sufficient to lead rational people to want to do away with it and to replace it with a system without exploitation, one based upon human needs?

Marx did not think that there was anything so automatic about a movement to end capitalism. People may struggle against specific aspects of capitalism—they may struggle over the workday, the level of wages and working conditions, capital's destruction of the environment, etc.—but unless they understand the nature of the system, they are struggling merely for a *nicer* capitalism, a capitalism with a human face. They are engaged merely, Marx stressed, "in a guerrilla war against the effects of the existing system" rather than in a war trying to abolish it.

In fact, nothing was clearer for Marx than the way capital maintains its hegemony, the way the rule of capital is reproduced. It continues to rule because people come to view capital as necessary. Because it looks like capital makes the major contribution to society, that without capital—no jobs, no income, no life. Every aspect of the social productivity of workers necessarily appears as the social productivity of *capital*. And, there is nothing accidental about this appearance. Marx commented that the transposition of "the social productivity of labor into the material attributes of capital is so firmly entrenched in people's minds that the advantages of machinery, the use of science, invention, etc., are *necessarily* conceived in this *alienated* form, so that all these things are deemed to be the *attributes of capital*."

Why? At the core of all this mystification of capital, this *inherent* mystification, is that central characteristic of capitalism, that act wherein the worker surrenders his or her creative power to the capitalist for a mess of pottage— the sale of the worker's capacity to labor to the capitalist. When we observe that transaction, Marx noted, it never appears as if workers have received the equivalent of their necessary labor and have performed surplus labor for the capitalist over and above that. The contract doesn't say—this is the portion of the day necessary for you to maintain yourself at the existing standard. Rather, on the surface, it *necessarily* looks like workers sell a certain quantity of labor, their entire workday, and get a wage that is (more or less) a fair return for their contribution—that they are paid, in short, for *all* the labor they perform. *How else could it possibly look?* In short, it necessarily appears as if the worker is not exploited—as if profits come from somewhere else.

Profits, it seems to follow, must come from the contribution of the capitalist. It's not only workers—the capitalist *also* makes a contribution and receives its equivalent. We all get what we (and our assets) deserve. (Some people just happen to make so much more of a contribution and so deserve that much more!) There you have the apologetic wisdom of the economists, who (as Marx noted) simply codify these appearances in elaborate formulas and equations. Nothing, though, is easier to understand than why this mystification occurs—given the form that the sale of labor-power necessarily takes on the surface. It is the source of "all the notions of justice held by both worker and capitalist, all the mystifications of the capitalist mode of production, all capitalism's illusions about freedom."

Further, insofar as profits are deemed not to be the result of exploitation but to flow from the contribution of the capitalist, it necessarily follows that accumulated capital must not be the result of the workers' own product but rather comes from the capitalist's own sacrifice in abstaining from consuming all his profits—it is the effect of "the self-chastisement of this modern penitent of Vishnu, the capitalist." Capital, in short, appears entirely independent of workers, appears as an independent source of wealth (and all the more so, the more that science and social productivity appear in the form of fixed capital).

It cannot be surprising, then, if workers look upon capital as the goose that lays the golden eggs and conclude that meeting the needs of capital is simply common sense. By its very nature, capitalism generates the appearance that there is no alternative. As Marx indicated:

> The advance of capitalist production develops a working class which by
> education, tradition, and habit looks upon the requirements of that mode

as self-evident natural laws. The organization of the capitalist process of production, once it is fully developed, breaks down all resistance.[5]

It is this acceptance of capital that ensures the continuing reproduction of the system. Clearly, Marx did not think that replacing capitalism would be easy.

Going Beyond Capitalism

Yet, Marx did think replacing capitalism was possible. Precisely because of the inherent mystification of capital, Marx wrote *Capital*, the culmination of his life's study. He believed it was essential to explain to workers the true nature of capital, important enough to "sacrifice my health, happiness, and family." Marx, in short, wrote *Capital* as a political act, as part of his revolutionary project.

In order to understand what capital is, he stressed, you have to go beneath the surface and try to grasp the underlying hidden structure of the system. You can never understand capitalism by looking at the parts of the system separately. And, by focusing on competition, you won't understand the inner dynamics of the system; it means you will be lost in appearances, the way the inner laws necessarily appear to the actors, and will not ask the right questions. Rather, you need to consider the system as a whole and to ask: How does this system reproduce itself? Where do the elements necessary for its reproduction come from? In short, where do the capitalists and wage-laborers necessary for capitalist relations of production come from?

What Marx demonstrated by examining capitalism as a reproducing system was that the capital that stands opposite the worker is not an unexplained premise (as it necessarily appears) but can be grasped as the result of previous exploitation, the result of previous extractions of surplus value. This same perspective of considering the system as one that must reproduce its own premises points to the shallowness of the view that wages reflect the contribution of workers to the production process. If workers simply are selling a quantity of labor and getting its equivalent, what ensures that they secure enough in return to be able to reproduce themselves? What, indeed, ensures that they don't (as a group) get enough to save up and *escape* from wage-labor? How does this system sustain itself?

By analyzing the system as a whole, Marx demystified the nature of capital. Enter into the logic of his analysis, and you can no longer look at capital as this wondrous god providing us with sustenance in return for our periodic sacrifices. Rather, you understand capital as the product of working people, our own power turned against us. Marx's focus upon the whole, in short, illustrates that the point is not to reform this or that bad side of capitalism but the need to do away with the antihuman system that is capitalism.

It didn't mean that Marx attempted to discourage workers from struggling for reforms. On the contrary, he argued that not to struggle for themselves on a daily basis leaves workers "apathetic, thoughtless, more or less well-fed instruments of production." Marx's consistent theme was that of the importance of revolutionary practice, the simultaneous changing of circumstances and self-change. By struggling against capital to satisfy their needs, workers produce themselves in ways that prepare them for a new society; they come to recognize the need to understand the nature of the system and to realize that they *cannot* limit themselves to guerrilla wars against the effects of the existing system. And, that, as Marx knew, is the point when capitalism can no longer be sustained.

The society to which Marx looked as an alternative to capitalism was one in which the relation of production would be that of an association of free producers. Freely associated individuals would treat "their communal, social productivity as their social wealth," producing for the needs of all. They would produce themselves as members of a truly human community—one that permits the full development of human potential. In contrast to capitalist society "in which the worker exists to satisfy the need of the existing values for valorization" (as a means for the growth of capital), this would be "the inverse situation, in which objective wealth is there to satisfy the worker's own need for development."[6] In such a society, "the free development of each is the condition for the free development of all."

2

Ideology and Economic Development

Economic theory is not neutral, and the results when it is applied owe much to the implicit and explicit assumptions embedded in a particular theory.[1] That such assumptions reflect specific ideologies is most obvious in the case of the neoclassical economics that underlies neoliberal economic policies.

The Magic of Neoclassical Economics

Neoclassical economics begins with the premises of private property and self-interest. Whatever the structure and distribution of property rights, it assumes the right of owners—whether as owners of land, means of production, or the capacity to perform labor—to follow their self-interest. In short, neither the interests of the community as such nor the development of human potential are the subject matter of neoclassical economics; its focus, rather, is upon the effects of decisions made by individuals with respect to their property.

Logically, then, the basic unit of analysis for this theory is the individual. This individual (whether a consumer, employer, or worker) is assumed to be a rational computer, an automaton mechanically maximizing its benefit on the basis of given data. Change the data and this "lightning calculator of pleasures and pains" (in the words of the American economist Thorstein Veblen) quickly selects a new optimum position.[2]

Raise the price of a commodity, and the computer as consumer chooses less of it. Raise the wage, and the computer as capitalist chooses to substitute machinery for workers. Raise unemployment or welfare benefits, and the computer as worker chooses to stop working or to remain unemployed longer. Increase taxes on profits, and the computer as capitalist chooses to invest elsewhere. In every case, the question asked is, how will that individual, the rational calculator of pleasure and pain, react to a change in the data? And, the answer is always self-evident—avoid pain, seek pleasure. Also self-evident are the inferences to be drawn from this simple theory—if you want to have less unemployment, you should lower wages, reduce unemployment and welfare benefits, and cut taxes on capital.

But, how does this theory move from its basic unit of the isolated, atomistic computer to draw inferences for society as a whole? The essential proposition of the theory is that the whole is the sum of the individual isolated parts. So, if we know how individuals respond to various stimuli, we know how the society composed of those individuals will respond. (In the words of Margaret Thatcher, there is no such thing as society—just individuals.) What is true for the individual is true for the economy as a whole. Further, since each economy can be considered as an individual—one who can compete and prosper internationally by driving down wages, intensifying work, removing social benefits that reduce the intensity of job searches, lowering the costs of government, and cutting taxes—it therefore follows that all economies can, too.

To move from the individual to the whole in this manner, though, involves a basic assumption. After all, those individual atomistic computers may work at cross-purposes; the result of individual rationality may be collective irrationality. So why isn't this the conclusion of neoclassical economics? Because *faith* bars that path—the belief that when those automatons are moved in one direction or another by the change in given data, they necessarily find the most efficient solution for all. In its early versions the religious aspect was quite explicit—that instantaneous calculator of individual pleasure and pain was understood to be "led by an invisible hand to promote an end which was no part of his intention."[3] For Adam Smith it was clear whose hand that was—Nature, Providence, God—just as his physiocratic contemporary, François Quesnay, knew that "the Supreme Being" was the source of this "principle of economic harmony," this "magic" being such that "each man works for others, while believing that he is working for himself."[4]

But the Supreme Being is no longer acknowledged as the author of this magic. In his place stands the Market, whose commandments all must follow or face its wrath. The unfettered market, we are told, ensures that everyone benefits from a free exchange (or it would not occur) and that those trades chosen by rational individuals (from all possible exchanges) will produce the best possible outcomes. Accordingly, it follows that interference with the perfect market by the state must produce disaster—a negative-sum result in which the losses exceed the gains. So, the answer for all right-thinking people must be, remove these interferences. In John Kenneth Galbraith's well-chosen words, the position of the fundamentalist preachers is that in a state of bliss, there is no need for a Ministry of Bliss.[5]

And, if force and compulsion are necessary to bring about that world of bliss (i.e., to make the world conform to the theory), this will simply be "short-term pain for long-term gain." As Friedrich von Hayek explained in an interview for Chile's *El Mercurio* (April 12, 1981), dictatorship "may be a necessary system for a transition period. At times it is necessary for a country that there is some form of dictatorial power." When you have the invisible hand on your side, destroying obstacles to the market is just helping Nature (in Adam Smith's words) to remedy the "bad effects of the folly and injustice of man."[6]

So, remove all restrictions on the movement of capital, remove all laws that strengthen workers, consumers, and citizens against capital, and reduce the power of the state to check capital (while increasing the power of the state to police *on behalf of* capital). In the end, the simple message of neoclassical economics (and the neoliberal policy it supports) is, Let capital be free!

Of course, it can be said (and, indeed, was said by Joseph Stiglitz) that nobody believes this simple message anymore. After all, economists have demonstrated the very strict (and impossible) conditions necessary for this theory to be logically supportable, have exposed the simplistic theory of information it contains, and have revealed the many cases of "market failure" that call for an ameliorating role for government. Not the least of these common critiques stresses the interdependencies and externalities that are minimized by neoclassical theorists and often lead them to commit fallacies of composition (the assumption that what is true for one is necessarily true for all). And yet, as the close fit between the simple neoclassical model and neoliberal policies demonstrates, all these sophisticated partial critiques of the simple message don't count for very much; in fact, that message (even if "defunct") continues to be believed, and it functions as a weapon to be used on behalf of capital.

The Keynesian Alternative

The only successful challenge from within this basic model focused on the problem of the fallacy of composition and, accordingly, the need to consider the importance of the whole. Rejecting the familiar neoclassical argument offered during the Great Depression of the 1930s that generalized wage cuts would lead to rising employment, Keynes stressed the interdependence of wages, consumption spending, aggregate demand, and thus the general level of output and employment. (The neoclassical movement from the part to the whole in this case, he held, depended upon the assumption that aggregate demand was constant—i.e., unaffected by wage cuts.) What neoclassical theory had ignored was the link between individual decisions and the whole. Since it did not understand how the interaction of individual capitals could produce a state of low investment by those capitals, it failed to recognize the potential role of government in remedying this particular market failure.

With his emphasis upon the whole or macro picture, Keynes's theoretical perspective provided support for a set of policies less directly based upon the immediate interests of individual capitals. Keynes himself advanced his arguments as critical to the interests of capital as a whole—the crisis of the 1930s for him was simply a crisis of "intelligence"; however, his framework became the basis for social-democratic policy arguments.[7]

Characteristic of the use of the Keynesian macro framework was the familiar argument by trade unionists that increased wages would increase aggregate demand, and stimulate job creation and new investment. The importance of increased consumption became the focus of what has been described somewhat misleadingly as the "Fordist" model of development—mass consumption, it was argued, is necessary for mass production.[8] However, to realize these benefits the market by itself would not suffice—state policies and macromanagement were seen as critical. What marked this as social democratic in essence was the consistent theme that workers could gain without capital losing—these positive-sum claims characterized the Fordist model. And what the case for endogenous (internally oriented) economic development has shared with the Fordist model is its stress upon the importance of domestic demand as the foundation for the development of nationally based industry.

During the "golden age" between the end of the Second World War and the early 1970s, these theories, which challenged the neoclassical wisdom, enjoyed a period of grace. It was an unusual period: the United States had emerged from the war with no real capitalist competitors—the economies of Germany and Japan were basket cases, and the industries of France, England, and Italy could not compete with those of the United States. Further, in the United States and elsewhere, there was considerable pent-up demand both from households and firms. Although it was widely predicted that the end of the war would bring a relapse into another depression, in fact the conditions were ripe for a substantial increase in consumption and investment (the latter drawing upon a large pool of technological advances made in the 1930s and 1940s). Added to that (and supporting industrial profits) were falling terms of trade for primary products as the result of increased supplies. In the United States, oligopolistic industries were able to engage in target pricing to achieve desired profit rates and could allow wage increases without fear of being uncompetitive; elsewhere, the economies of scale available from new investments made the growth of consumption as the result of wage increases a net benefit rather than a challenge to profitability.

Here was the setting in which the virtuous circle of the Fordist model could flourish: increased output stimulated gains in consumption and vice versa—in developed countries as well as those developing countries that decided to industrialize on the basis of import-substitution rather than rely on the fortunes of primary product exports. But the rapid growth of productive capacity in many places during the period portended a point when capital would face a problem of overaccumulation.

Already by the late 1950s, there were signs that competitors were emerging to challenge U.S. economic hegemony. Further, by the mid-1960s, terms of trade for primary products (dominated by oil) stopped falling, soon to begin an upward movement. Increasingly, it was the companies outside the United States that were growing more rapidly, and by the early 1970s, with falling profit rates spreading, the "golden age" of capitalism is generally conceded to have come to an end.

The increasing intensity of capitalist competition, which now became apparent, reflected the overaccumulation of capital. In this context, transnational firms reduced their production costs by shutting down some (relatively inefficient) branch plants that had been established to serve particular national markets and by turning others into exporters as part of a global production strategy. Production for national markets and thus the import-substitution strategy for industrialization was now no longer seen as credible because relative costs became the focus in the competition of capitals. In general, the virtuous circle of Fordism had been broken, and a premium was placed instead on driving down wages and other costs for capital.

This "new reality" is the context in which Keynesianism was rejected. The neoclassical wisdom, which identified high wages and social programs as sources of disaster, once again dominated. Neoliberalism (supported by international financial institutions) became the weapon of choice of capital, leading to a generalized assault on social programs, wages, and working conditions in the developed world and the use of a strong state in developing countries to ensure their access to the comparative advantage of repression.

But why were Keynesianism and the Fordist model so easily discredited? Basically, Keynesianism as transmitted was always a theory of aggregate

demand but not of supply. Its premise was that the level of output is con-
strained by demand in the economy in question; and if that demand is forth-
coming, capital will provide the supply. Since the assumption was that capital
would supply the consumption and investment goods if government created
the appropriate environment, the government's role was to stimulate the economy in those cases where the interaction of individual capitals would otherwise lead to low investment. Its assigned task in the theory was to create the
environment for investment when the market failed.

What happened, though, when aggregate demand rose and domestic
supply did *not* respond appropriately? Inflation and trade deficits increased.
Accordingly, in the new reality, the environment that government sought to
create became one that would induce investment in the local economy rather
than investment *elsewhere*—its focus became to lower taxes and wages. The
neoclassical and Keynesian question, in short, had remained the same: What
can the state do to make capital happy to invest? What was consistent was
the role envisioned for government—support capital's requirements.

The Failure of Social Democracy

There should be no surprise, then, that capital abandoned the tool of
Keynesian theory for one more suited to its needs under the new conditions. But how do we explain the failure of social democracy to find an
alternative? After all, social democracy has always presented itself as pro-
ceeding from a logic in which the needs and potentialities of human beings
take priority over the needs of capital. Even limited measures such as the
exclusion of medical and educational services from the market, the provi-
sion of income maintenance programs and social services, and the advoca-
cy of everyone's right to a decent and well-paying job suggest an implicit
conception of wealth as the satisfaction of human needs—rather than one of
capitalist wealth.

In fact, the failure of Keynesianism as theory was really the failure of an
ideology—social democracy. Within the Keynesian structure, there was

always an alternative. The basic Keynesian equations in themselves say nothing about the structure of the economy; they don't distinguish between burying money and government investment, between activity that leads to the expansion of capitalist enterprises and activity that leads to the expansion of state enterprises. Although for Keynes the appropriate engine for growth was the capitalist one, a policy of expanding a state productive sector was always a theoretical option in order to drive the economy.

If the capitalist sector is the only sector identified for accumulation, however, then in theory and practice the implication is self-evident: a "capital strike" is a crisis for the economy. All other things equal, a government cannot encroach upon capital without negative-sum results. This has always been the wisdom of conservative economists.

Yet it is essential to understand that the conclusions of the neoclassical economists are embedded in their assumptions—and particularly relevant here is the assumption that all other things are equal. Consider two simple examples, rent control and mineral royalties.[9] If you introduce rent controls (at an effective level), the conservative economist predicts that the supply of rental housing will dry up and a housing shortage will emerge. Likewise, he will tell us that if you attempt to tax resource rents (notoriously difficult to estimate), investment and production in these sectors will decline, generating unemployment. Both those propositions can be easily demonstrated—and they can also easily be demonstrated to be entirely fallacious with respect to the necessary conclusion.

Assumed constant in both cases is the character and level of government activity. Clearly, rent controls may reduce private rental construction—but if the government simultaneously engages in the development of social housing programs (e.g., the fostering of cooperatives and other forms of nonprofit housing), there is no necessary emergence of a housing shortage. Similarly, taxing resource revenues may dry up private investment in mineral exploration, but a government corporation established for exploration and production in this sector can counteract the effects of a capital strike. Obviously, all other things are not *necessarily* equal. Why should all other things be equal if a social democratic government rejects the logic of capital?

Thus we need to be aware of the limits of the conservative economist's logic. However, that does not at all mean that these arguments can be ignored! Because what the conservative economist does quite well is indicate what capital will do in response to particular measures. It is an economics of capital. And nothing is more naive than to assume that you can undertake certain measures of economic policy *without* a response from capital; nothing is more certain to backfire than introducing measures that serve people's needs without anticipating capital's response. Those who do not respect the conservative economist's logic, which is the logic of capital, and incorporate it into their strategy are doomed to constant surprises and disappointments.

Understanding the responses of capital means that a capital strike can be an opportunity rather than a crisis. If you reject dependence upon capital, the logic of capital can be revealed clearly as contrary to the needs and interests of people. When capital goes on strike, there are two choices, *give in* or *move in*. Unfortunately, social democracy in practice has demonstrated that it is limited by the same things that limit Keynesianism in theory—the givens of the structure and distribution of ownership and the priority of self-interest by the owners. As a result, when capital has gone on strike, the social-democratic response has been to give in.

Rather than maintaining its focus on human needs and challenging the logic of capital, social democracy has proceeded to enforce that logic. The result has been the discrediting of Keynesianism and the ideological disarming of people who looked upon it as an alternative to the neoclassical wisdom. The only alternative to the barbarism being offered became barbarism with a human face. With this acquiescence to the logic of capital, its hold over people was reinforced; and the political result was the popular conclusion either that it really doesn't matter *who* you elect or that the real solution is to be found in a government *unequivocally* committed to the logic of capital.

So it was that the new wisdom became TINA—There Is No Alternative. No alternative to neoliberalism, which is simply neoclassical economics enforced by finance capital and imperialist power. Yet, as occurred after the "golden age," concrete conditions have a way of undermining accepted truths

—and nowhere has this been truer than in less developed countries. The fallacy of assuming that every country could become the promised land by surrendering completely to capital became clear; and, as the evidence of the failures of the external orientation imposed by neoliberalism has accumulated, interest in an internal solution, the endogenous model of development, has grown again—especially in Latin America. Yet how credible is such an option in the current conjuncture where intense capitalist competition continues and the power of international capital in fact (if not ideology) has not declined?

The Possibility of Endogenous Development

Removing the straitjacket placed upon economic development by neoliberalism will not be an easy matter. A true focus upon endogenous development cannot simply be an orientation to the limited markets that characterized previous import-substitution efforts; rather, it calls for incorporating the mass of the population that has been excluded from their share of the achievements of modern civilization. In short, real endogenous development means making real the preferential option for the poor. And that means making enemies— internally (both those who monopolize the land and the wealth and those who are content with the status quo) and externally.

Any country that would challenge neoliberalism by seriously attempting to foster endogenous development will face the assorted weapons of international capital—foremost among them the International Monetary Fund, the World Bank, finance capital, and imperialist power (including such forms as the U.S. National Endowment for Democracy and other forces of subversion). These are, of course, formidable foes. Since no government based simply on its own resources can hope to succeed in this struggle against such internal and external enemies, the central question will be whether the government is willing to mobilize its people on behalf of the policies that meet the needs of people. Here the essential matter is the extent to which the government has freed itself from the ideological domination of capital.

This unshackling implies more than simply a return to the old idea of import-substitute industrialization—even if accompanied this time by the massive land reform that would create the potential for a much larger home market. New models of Keynesianism—even dressed up as the Fordist positive-sum solution—will not move those whose active support will be necessary to strengthen the resolve of a government that will find itself constantly pressured by capital to sue for peace. Theories that continue to be rooted in existing patterns of ownership, in the dominating principle of self-interest, and in the belief that (outside of a few exceptions) the market knows best, cannot support a successful challenge to the logic of capital—they are an organic part of that logic.

The central flaw in social democratic proposals for endogenous development is that they break neither ideologically nor politically with dependence upon capital. If a model of endogenous development is to be successful, it must base itself upon a theory that places the goal of human development first. More than the consumption stressed by neoclassicals and Keynesians alike, it must focus on investment in and development of human capacities. This means not only the investments in human beings that come from the direction of expenditures and human activity to the critical areas of education and health (i.e., what has been called investment in "human capital") but also from the real development of human potential which occurs as the result of human activity. This is the essence of the revolutionary practice that Marx described, the simultaneous changing of circumstances and human activity or self-change.[10] In contrast to a populism that merely promises new consumption, this alternative model focuses upon new production—the transformation of people through their own activity, the building of human capacities.

A development theory that begins from the recognition of human beings as productive forces points in quite a different direction than that of the economics of capital. Where are the measures in traditional theory for the self-confidence that arises in people through the conscious development of cooperation and democratic problem-solving in communities and workplaces? Where is the focus upon the potential efficiency gains of unleashing these human productive forces, whose creativity and tacit knowledge cannot be produced by directives from capital? By stimulating the solidarity that comes from an emphasis upon the interests of the community rather than self-interest, a model based upon this radical supply-side theory rooted in human development will allow a government to move further with the support of the community. Within such a framework, the growth of noncapitalist sectors oriented to meeting people's needs is not merely a defense against a capital strike; rather, it emerges as an organic development. Here, human needs and capacities, rather than the needs of capital, become the engine that drives the economy.

Endogenous development is possible—but only if a government is prepared to break ideologically and politically with capital, only if it is prepared to make social movements actors in the realization of an economic theory based upon the concept of human capacities. In the absence of such a rupture, economically, the government will constantly find it necessary to stress the importance of providing incentives to private capital; and, politically, its central fear will be that of the "capital strike." The policies of such a government inevitably will disappoint and demobilize all those looking for an alternative to neoliberalism; and, once again, its immediate product will be the conclusion that there is no alternative.

3

The Knowledge of a Better World

There is an old saying that if you don't know where you want to go, then any road will take you there.[1] I think that recent years, years of neoliberalism, imperialist outrages, and the virtual destruction of almost every effort to create an alternative, have disproved this saying. Our experience tells us that if you don't know where you want to go, then *no* road will take you there.

Our greatest failing is that we have lost sight of an alternative. And, because we have no grand conception of an alternative (indeed, we are told that we *should* have no grand conceptions), then the response to the neoliberal mantra of TINA, that There Is No Alternative, has been: Let's preserve health care, let's not attack education, and let's try for a little more equality and a little more preservation of the environment. Because of our failure to envision an alternative as a whole, we have many small pieces, many small no's; indeed, the only feasible alternative to barbarism proposed has been barbarism with a human face.

Let us think about a real alternative to barbarism, a grand conception but yet a very simple one. I have in mind a simple idea expressed by Karl Marx in 1844 (but one which runs throughout his work): the unity of human beings based upon recognition of their differences. That is a conception which begins from the recognition that people are different—that they have differing needs and differing capabilities—and that they are interdependent.

Whether we act upon the basis of this understanding of our interdependence or not, we cannot deny that we produce for each other, that as beings within society, there is a chain of human activity that links us. We produce inputs for each other, and the ultimate result of our activity is the reproduction of human beings within society. We can think of this as the activity of a collective worker, as that of the human family, or as that of the family of workers, but this chain of human activity exists whether we consciously produce on this basis or not—whether we understand our unity or not.

In fact, as we know only too well, outside of little oases (some societies, some families) in this society we do *not* consciously produce for the needs of others, and we do not understand our productive activity as our contribution to this chain of human activity. Instead of valuing our relationship as human beings, we produce commodities, we value commodities; instead of understanding this chain of human activity as our bond and our power, we understand only that we need these commodities, that we are dominated by them.

The Knowledge of Commodities

This, as is well-known, is what Marx called the "fetishism of commodities" in the first chapter of *Capital.* It is a powerful concept. In my view, no one has ever communicated this idea better than the artist Wallace Shawn, an actor and playwright from the United States. In his play *The Fever,* Shawn's protagonist at one point finds a copy of *Capital* and begins to read it at night. He thinks about the anger in this book, and then he goes back to the beginning, which he had initially found to be impenetrable. Here I'll quote a long passage from Wallace Shawn:

> I came to a phrase that I'd heard before, a strange, upsetting, sort of ugly phrase: this was the section on "commodity fetishism," "the fetishism of commodities." I wanted to understand that weird-sounding phrase, but I

could tell that, to understand it, your whole life would probably have to change.

His explanation was very elusive. He used the example that people say, "Twenty yards of linen are worth two pounds." People say that about everything, that it has a certain value. This is worth that. This coat, this sweater, this cup of coffee: each thing worth some quantity of money, or some number of other things—one coat, worth three sweaters, or so much money—as if that coat, suddenly appearing on the earth, contained somewhere inside itself an amount of value, like an inner soul, as if the coat were a fetish, a physical object that contains a living spirit. But what really determines the value of a coat? The coat's price comes from its history, the history of all the people involved in making it and selling it and all the particular relationships they had. And if we buy the coat, we, too, form relationships with all those people, and yet we hide those relationships from our own awareness by pretending we live in a world where coats have no history but just fall down from heaven with prices marked inside. "I like this coat," we say. "It's not expensive," as if that were a fact about the *coat* and not the end of a story about all the people who made it and sold it. "I like the pictures in this magazine."

A naked woman leans over a fence. A man buys a magazine and stares at her picture. The destinies of these two are linked. The man has paid the woman to take off her clothes, to lean over the fence. The photograph contains its history—the moment the woman unbuttoned her shirt, how she felt, what the photographer said. The price of the magazine is a code that describes the relationships between all these people—the woman, the man, the publisher, the photographer—who commanded, who obeyed. The cup of coffee contains the history of the peasants who picked the beans, how some of them fainted in the heat of the sun, some were beaten, some were kicked.

For two days I could see the fetishism of commodities everywhere around me. It was a strange feeling. Then on the third day I lost it, it was gone, I couldn't see it anymore.[2]

In this quotation from Wallace Shawn a certain type of knowledge is described—price. Price is the form in which that chain of human activity and human relationships appears to us. This knowledge comes in monetary units. We know the prices of the things we need. We know the price we have ourselves received. And, now we must take that knowledge and make individual rational decisions, as consumers, as capitalists—we're all the same: maximizers on the basis of the knowledge we have, maximizers on the basis of money.

Think about the knowledge we do *not* have in this world where money is the medium of knowledge. We know about nothing that does not come to us with a price—the natural environment around us, our own needs for the development of our potential; we know nothing about the lives of all those people who have produced the things we purchase, all those people with whom we have entered into a relationship by buying the results of their activity. Our situation is one of social ignorance, and that very ignorance is what permits us to be divided, turned against each other, and exploited by the owners of commodities, the owners of the chain of human activity.

When our knowledge is the price of things, how can we avoid being divided? When we don't recognize our unity, how can we avoid competing against each other to the benefit of the owners of knowledge?

Another Kind of Knowledge

Think about another kind of knowledge—a knowledge based upon recognition of our unity, knowledge based upon a concept of solidarity. It is a different knowledge when we are aware of who produces for us and how, when we understand the conditions of life of others and the needs they have for what we can contribute. Knowledge of this type immediately places us as beings within society, provides an understanding of the basis of all our lives. It is immediately direct social knowledge because it cannot be communicated through the indirect medium of money.

Knowledge of our needs and capacities is radical because it goes to the root, to human beings. And when it is obtained because we recognize our unity, it is knowledge that differs qualitatively and quantitatively from the knowledge we have under the dominant social relations. It is quantitatively different because existing relations no longer make its monopolization and restriction a source of private gain. It is inherent in knowledge that it is a public good. Knowledge can be reproduced at almost no cost, and unlike scarce commodities, I do not have less knowledge if I give you some of mine. In a rational society, knowledge should be shared without any restriction.

The existence of institutions that make knowledge property and a source of private gain, then, are contrary to the concept and ethos of knowledge and demonstrate the social irrationality of those institutions. Take the grading mechanism in many universities, for example. It is a common practice for professors in North America to grade according to a normal statistical curve—so many A's, B's, C's, D's, and F's—regardless of overall student performance. What kind of behavior does this make rational for those who function within such a structure? Clearly, it is to keep knowledge to themselves (or to a small subset of friends). The more other students know, the lower are one's own chances for a good grade. (In fact, it makes it rational to give other students *false* information.) The structure in this case puts students in competition—a situation that Robert Wyatt, the British singer, once sang about with the line, "How can I rise, if you don't fall?" This artificially created structure produces a zero-sum game in the case of knowledge which, by its very nature, is *not* zero-sum. Thus, whereas ideally a university might be viewed as an environment dedicated to the fullest possible development and dissemination of knowledge—something that a collective learning process would encourage—we can see that the creation of an environment that rewards private ownership of knowledge is contrary to the idealized concept of the university.

In many respects, this can be seen as a parable of intellectual property rights. What intellectual property rights do is to attempt to create an artificial scarcity that will compel people to pay more for knowledge than its actual cost of reproduction. The purpose is to make what Marx called the products of the social brain a source of private enrichment. In a society, on the other hand, which begins from the recognition of the needs of all its members, the logical and rational impulse is to make knowledge available to all at its true cost of reproduction—zero.

Where our social relations and institutions are not such as to lead us to view our knowledge as property, there is another way by which the knowledge available to all is expanded. Much knowledge is not codified; it is "tacit knowledge"—knowledge, e.g., of how work could be done better, knowledge of how it could be easier. Within antagonistic productive relations, the situation especially of the wage-laborer, this is knowledge to be kept to yourself—in order to ensure that it is not used against you. In a rational society, it is knowledge we would share. "Gold in the workers' heads" is what Japanese labor relations experts called it when they introduced mechanisms to induce workers to share ideas about improving products and production processes. This knowledge is wealth that would flow naturally in a society based upon the recognition of our interdependence.

Tacit knowledge is an example of a type of knowledge available freely under a different set of social relations. It is not, however, the only difference in the knowledge that would be available. When we begin from the conception of an alternative society, it becomes clear that a certain type of knowledge is hidden from us under our existing relations. The knowledge not communicated in a commodity economy is that which has no price in the market. The natural environment in which we live, the air we breathe, the sights we see, the sounds we hear, the water we drink (ah, *once* the water we drank) has no price and thus does not enter into our monetary calculus. And without that price, it is invisible when we as atomistic maximizers make our decisions. It means that these decisions, based upon partial knowledge, are inherently biased. If we were able to place an appropriate price upon clean air, our actions as calculating producers and consumers would produce different decisions—ones more likely to ensure the maintenance of clean air. Hypothetically, too, if we were able to place a price upon the full development of human potential or upon the ability to live in a just society, faced with this altered set of prices, our individual decisions would differ (as would the decisions of those who currently purchase our abilities without the need to consider their real price).

But how, in the absence of commodity exchanges, can such information that takes into account what Marx called "the worker's own need for development" be generated? If we share Marx's emphasis upon the importance of the rich human being, "the totally developed individual," then certainly we must concern ourselves with the mechanisms by which the knowledge of needs and capabilities can be produced.

The Accumulation of Knowledge for Human Development

Those who are here to discuss ways to defend humanity against the barbarism it currently faces begin from certain values. These values are embodied in the constitution of the Bolivarian Republic of Venezuela—in the goal described in Article 299 of "ensuring overall human development," in the declaration of Article 20 that "everyone has the right to the free development of his or her own personality," and in the focus of Article 102 upon "developing the creative potential of every human being and the full exercise of his or her personality in a democratic society."

That constitution also is quite specific on how this human development occurs: participation. Much like Marx's stress upon human activity as the way people transform both circumstances and themselves, Article 62 of the Bolivarian constitution declares that participation by people is "the necessary way of achieving the involvement to ensure their complete development, both individual and collective." Human development, in short, does not drop from the sky—it is the result of a process, of *many* processes, in which people transform themselves. It is the product of a society which is "democratic, participatory, and protagonistic" (to quote the constitution once again).

Through social forms (as set out in Article 70) such as "self-management, co-management, cooperatives in all forms," through democratic planning and participatory budgeting at all levels of society, people develop their capabilities and capacities. This process of transformative activity, though, is precisely the process of developing the knowledge required for this alternative society. That information cannot come from markets, from surveys, nor negotiations at the top—it comes neither from the fetishism of commodities nor the fetishism of the plan. It is through democratic discussions and decisions at every level that we can identify our needs and our capabilities. The creation of democratic institutions is precisely the way in which we expand the quality and quantity of knowledge that can make a society based upon unity and the recognition of difference work. How else can we understand the needs of others except by hearing their voices? How else can we consciously insert ourselves in the chain of human activity? The knowledge needed to build and sustain an alternative society, a society based upon human bonds, is necessarily "democratic, participatory, and protagonistic."

The Battle of Ideas

Knowing where we want to go is a necessity if we want to build an alternative. But, it is not the same as being there. We live in a world dominated by global capital, a world in which capital divides us, setting the people of each country against each other to see who can produce more cheaply by driving wages, working conditions, and environmental standards to the lowest level in order to survive in the war of all against all. We know, too, that any country that would challenge neoliberalism faces the assorted weapons of international capital—foremost among them the IMF, the World Bank, and imperialist power (in various forms including the U.S. National Endowment for Democracy and other forces of subversion).

The most immediate obstacle, though, is the belief in TINA. Without the vision of a better world, every crisis of capitalism (such as the one upon us) can bring in the end only a painful restructuring—with the pain felt by those already exploited and excluded. The concept of an alternative, of a society based upon solidarity, is an essential weapon in defense of humanity. We need to recognize the possibility of a world in which the products of the social brain and the social hand are common property and the basis for our self-development—the possibility in Marx's words of "a society of free individuality, based on the universal development of individuals and on their subordination of their communal, social productivity as their social wealth."[3] For this reason, the battle of ideas is essential.

That battle can be fought in many ways. For one, it points to the importance of the deepening of the real process in societies where the beginnings of an alternative have been made. The glimpses of a better world that they provide—even in the midst of concerted attacks by imperialism—are an inspiration for struggles everywhere around the world, a demonstration that there is an alternative.

But it is only in those struggles themselves that we spread an understanding of that alternative. These are struggles that start from people's needs, from their discontent over the gap between what society promises them and what they are able to obtain. The battle of ideas begins here by communicating knowledge of the nature of capitalism—by demonstrating that poverty is not the fault of the poor, that exclusion is not the fault of the excluded, that wealth is the result of the chain of human activity.

These struggles, too, are explicitly about knowledge—the struggles against property rights that deny free access to the intellectual accomplishments of humanity. They are struggles against commodification, against the invasion of money and price into all aspects of life. But they are also struggles for new democratic forms that are a means of tapping the gold in the heads of all people and of communicating all our needs and capacities. They are struggles, in short, for a democratic, participatory, and protagonistic alternative.

In this era of capitalist globalization and neoliberalism, however, it is obvious that more than local democratic institutions are needed. How can we understand the needs and capacities of people who are geographically distant but intimately close as parts of the human chain of activity? How can we see other limbs of the collective worker as human beings with needs rather than as competitors? We develop our understanding of our unity and interdependence with those who capitalist globalization has assembled around the world through solidarity with those people—not only with their specific struggles as workers or citizens but also by linking up with them directly on the basis of community to community.

To build a world based upon solidarity, we must practice solidarity—and in that way transform both circumstances and ourselves. If we know where we want to go and we know what is necessary to get there, we have begun the battle to defend humanity against barbarism.

Finally, to take up a theme introduced last night by President Chávez and Pablo González Casanova about the need to make real changes in the world, let me close by paraphrasing Marx, using the language appropriate to this conference: the idea of human society is sufficient to defeat the idea of barbarism. But it takes real human action to defeat real barbarism.

4

Reclaiming a Socialist Vision

In the wake of Seattle and other dramatic displays of opposition to capitalist globalization, many people are now talking about capitalism and describing themselves as anti-capitalist.[1] Great! But what do they mean? That capital's international institutions are bad because they usurp the right of citizens to make democratic decisions? That financial speculation detracts from real, productive investment that creates real jobs? That the drive for profits on the part of transnational corporations has led them to ally with and strengthen authoritarian regimes that deny human rights? That neoliberal policies are producing a race to the bottom in terms of wages, working conditions, and environmental standards? These are all important to oppose—but in and by itself this is an opposition to specific policies and practices of capitalism rather than to capitalism as such.

Don't we need a vision of an alternative to capitalism? No one would deny there are some examples of capitalism that are better than others—largely as the result of the struggles of workers and peoples' movements to change things. Whether those examples have been the result of unique historical circumstances, whether by their very nature they cannot be generalized to the whole world, whether they are sustainable (especially in the context of global capitalism in a world of uneven development) is not the central question.

Rather, we need to ask: *Is that all there is?* Is there no alternative to an economic system that relies upon the propertylessness of the mass of people to compel them to work to produce profits for those who do own? Is there no alternative to a system in which the foundations of human wealth, human beings and nature, are treated as mere means for the generation of private monetary wealth, means often destroyed in the process? Is there no alternative to a system whose very logic is to divide and separate people, to preclude the possibilities for human solidarity?

Many people say, simply, *there is no alternative*. And, because there is none, the best we can do is try to make improvements here and there in capitalism. The belief that the only real alternative is capitalism with a human face owes much to the two great failures of the twentieth century: the experiences in those underdeveloped countries that strove for rapid industrialization through a hierarchical system they called socialist (with which few people in the more developed world can identify) and the failure of social democratic governments (some calling themselves socialist) in the developed world to do any more than tinker with capitalism as an economic system.

Why should we accept that these examples exhaust the potential for alternatives to capitalism? From the beginning of capitalism, people have seen in it a system that is destructive of human values and have looked to alternatives that would make our common humanity the core of social and economic relations. Not only in the utopias and visions of the nineteenth century but also in the experiments of the twentieth century are there glimpses and real examples that point to an alternative logic to that of capital, a logic based upon human beings. But that's not all—in the daily struggles against the logic of capital, that alternative logic is present (even if it is only implicit). What we need to do is to begin to reclaim and build that alternative vision—and to make what is implicit in those struggles explicit. Once we do that, too, the limitations of anti-capitalism by itself become clear.

Early Visions

Think about utopia—about the island of Utopia, to be exact. Thomas More's *Utopia* was written in sixteenth-century England, when medieval peasants were losing their traditional access to the land as the result of land being enclosed for sheep pasture. The mythical alternative More sketches is a society where land is held in common, where all are expected to do their fair share of work, and where the products of labor are distributed to all in accordance with their needs without money and without exchange. How can there be justice and prosperity, More asks, "when possessions are private, where money is the measure of all things?"

Such themes of common property, cooperation, equality, and the rejection of exchange relations accompanied many criticisms of capitalism as it developed in the eighteenth and early-nineteenth centuries in Western Europe. They were, in particular, part of the rejection of the changes that capitalism was bringing to rural society. Growing inequality and competition and the desire to profit at the expense of others were identified as the product of private property and the source of a disintegration of existing social links. The proposal of alternatives, though, was not simply seen as the attempt to restore a pre-capitalist (idealized) past. Capitalism, with its competition and rivalry, was seen as both irrational and as inferior to a society based upon direct human cooperation.

Many of those who rejected capitalism, accordingly, argued for the importance of creating experiments that could demonstrate that a cooperative society based upon common ownership of the means of production would be superior to capitalism. (The large amounts of land available in North America as the result of European conquest and settlement in fact permitted the establishment in the nineteenth century of a number of utopian communities embodying these principles and were seen as a way of revealing to all that there were viable alternatives to capitalism.) Similarly, the creation of cooperative workplaces in manufacturing also was advocated as a means of demonstrating the advantages of association and cooperation over the rivalry characteristic of capitalism. This latter development, though, reflected the further development of capitalism and a new and growing aspect of the opposition to capitalism—the rejection of its effects upon workers in industry, both those displaced by capitalist industry and those employed by it.

Increasingly in the nineteenth century (especially in England, where capitalism was most advanced), the opposition to capitalism became a workers' opposition, focusing upon the exploitation of workers. Labor, it was argued, was the source of all wealth in society; so how was it that workers grew poor on their wages while their masters grew rich? Clearly, part of the workers' product was taken by those who employed them. While some argued that workers should instead work for themselves in cooperative workshops (established either by themselves or by the state as social workshops) and should compete against capitalist firms, this was a position firmly rejected by the most important and influential socialist theorist of the nineteenth century, Karl Marx.

True, for Marx the cooperative factories that were established demonstrated that the subordination of workers to capital could be superseded by an association of free and equal producers. However, by themselves, those co-ops would remain "dwarfish" and would never transform capitalist society. What was necessary "to convert social production into one large and harmonious system of free and cooperative labor," Marx argued, was to change society as a whole—to transfer the existing means of production from capitalists and landlords to the producers themselves. In no sense, though, did Marx entirely reject the goals of his predecessors. The utopians had constructed (and propagandized around) "fantastic pictures and plans of a new society"; however, Marx argued that "only the means" of getting there are different: "The real conditions of the movement are no longer clouded in utopian fables." So, what were those goals ... and how were the means of getting there different?

The Goals and Means of Early Socialists

At the core of the goals of socialists was the creation of a society that would allow for the full development of human potential and capacity. The goal, as Henri Saint-Simon argued, is "to afford to all members of society the greatest possible opportunity for the development of their faculties." Similarly, real freedom, Louis Blanc proposed, is "the POWER given men to develop and exercise their faculties." And given that everyone "must have the *power* to develop and exercise his faculties in order to really be free, ... society owes every one of its members both instruction, without which the human mind *cannot* grow, and the instruments of labor, without which human activity *cannot* achieve its fullest development." This same theme was set out clearly by Friedrich Engels in the question-and-answer format of an early draft of the *Communist Manifesto*. Engels asks, "What is the aim of the Communists?" He answers, "To organize society in such a way that every member of it can develop and use all his capabilities and powers in complete freedom and without thereby infringing the basic conditions of this society." In the final version of the *Manifesto* (written by Marx), this goal was represented as "an association, in which the free development of each is the condition for the free development of all."

A less explicit statement, but there can be no question that the full development of human potential was at the very heart of Marx's conception of an alternative society—just as the stunting of that potential and the tendency to reduce human beings to beasts of burden and things was at the core of his rejection of capitalism. From his earliest writings, Marx stressed the potential for the development of rich human beings with rich human needs, the potential for producing human beings as rich as possible in needs and capabilities. What, indeed, is wealth, he asked, "other than the universality of individual needs, capacities, pleasures, productive forces...?" The prize was the "development of the rich individuality which is as all-sided in its production as in its consumption." Thus the growth of human wealth is "the absolute working out of his creative potentialities," the "development of all human powers as such the end in itself." Within capitalism, however, the goal of capital is def-

initely not the development of that potential. Rather, as Marx wrote in
Capital, the worker exists to satisfy the capitalist's need to increase the value
of his capital "as opposed to the inverse situation, in which objective wealth
is there to satisfy the worker's own need for development."

In the society of associated producers that Marx envisioned, the all-
sided development of people would be based upon "the subordination of
their communal, social productivity as their social wealth." Here increased
productivity would not come at the expense of workers but would translate
both into the satisfaction of needs and also the possibility of free time—
which "corresponds to the artistic, scientific, etc., development of the individuals in the time set free, and with the means created, for all of them." It
would be "time for the full development of the individual, which in turn
reacts back on the productive power of labor itself as itself the greatest productive power." All the springs of cooperative wealth would flow more abundantly, and the products of this society of freely associated producers would
be human beings able to develop their full potential in a human society.

So, how did Marx's conception of the means of going beyond capitalism
differ from those of his predecessors? As we have seen, for so many socialists
of the nineteenth century, the way to create the new society was to extract people from capitalism and to demonstrate that a non-capitalist alternative was a
superior form of social and economic arrangement; and those who argued this
often looked to philanthropists or the state to provide the funds for these new
demonstration projects. For Marx, however, such proposals reflected a time
when the horrors of capitalism were apparent but when capitalism had not yet
developed sufficiently to reveal "the real conditions of the movement."

Look to what working people are doing, Marx argued. Through their
own struggles to satisfy their needs (which, for Marx, reflect all aspects of
their existence as human beings within society and nature), they reveal that
the battle for a new society is conducted by struggling within capitalism
rather than by looking outside. In those struggles workers come to recognize
their common interests, they come to understand the necessity to join together against capital. It was not simply the formation of a bloc opposed to capi-

tal that emerges out of these struggles. Marx consistently stressed that the very process of struggle was a process of producing people in an altered way; in struggling for their needs, "they acquire a new need—the need for society—and what appears as a means becomes an end." They transform themselves into subjects capable of altering their world.

This is what Marx identified as "revolutionary practice"—"the coincidence of the changing of circumstances and human activity or self-change." Marx's message to workers, he noted at one point, was that you have to go through years of struggle "not only in order to bring about a change in society but also to change yourselves." Over twenty years later, he also wrote that workers know that "they will have to pass through long struggles, through a series of historic processes, transforming circumstances and men." In short, the means of achieving that new society were inseparable from the process of struggling for it—only in motion could people rid themselves of "all the muck of ages."

Socialism, for this reason, could never be delivered to people from above. It is the work of the working class itself, Marx argued. And that applied as well to the kind of democratic institutions workers need to bring about the new society. No state standing over and above society (and indeed crushing it like a boa constrictor—the way Marx described the French state) could be the basis for that simultaneous changing of circumstances and self-change. Only by rejecting hierarchy and converting the state "from an organ standing above society into one completely subordinate to it" could the state be that of "the popular masses themselves, forming their own force instead of the organized force of their suppression." Only that "self-government of the producers" could be the form of state by which people emancipate themselves and create the basis for a socialist society.

Reclaiming and Renewing a Socialist Vision

Certainly, the process of reclaiming a socialist vision involves the necessity to come to terms with the experiences of the twentieth century and its two great failures. But that process needs to begin somewhere. And where better than by recognizing, as Marx clearly did, that people develop through their activity and that a new society is inseparable from the new sides they take on in the struggle to satisfy their needs? How better than to return to a conception of socialism as a society in which the full development of human potential is paramount?

If we proceed explicitly from such a vision, then anti-capitalism is obviously part of that struggle. Who could imagine that the development of those rich human beings (rich because all-sided in their capacities and needs) is compatible with a society in which human beings and nature are mere means for the expansion of capital? At the same time, this vision of socialism clearly goes well beyond anti-capitalism as such and points to the limitations of a focus upon anti-capitalist struggle alone. Who these days could possibly think that the full development of human potential is compatible with patriarchy, racism, imperialism, or hierarchy, to name just a few sources of oppression? In the various struggles of people for human dignity and social justice, a vision of an alternative socialist society has always been latent. Let us reclaim and renew that vision.

5

Socialism Doesn't Drop from the Sky

Some people think you can change the world without taking power. No, they argue, you must not even think about trying to make use of the state.[1] Why? Because, as John Holloway asserts, "To struggle through the state is to become involved in the active process of defeating yourself." No, they proclaim, the state (by definition) cannot challenge capitalism. Why? Because it is part of capital; indeed, as Holloway writes, "The state (any state) must do everything it can to provide conditions that favor the profitability of capital."

Ideas like this are not new. But they have been revived in certain quarters (especially in Latin America) because they reflect a period of disappointment and defeat. Disappointment and defeat because of the failure of the state-dominated society of the Soviet Union and its followers to live up to its promises to create a new world; and disappointment and defeat because of the tragedy of social democracy, which through its surrender to the logic of capital, has demonstrated that it offers only barbarism with a human face.

Yet Holloway's insistence that we must reject "the very notion that society can be changed through the winning of state power" has been refuted in two clear ways. It has been refuted concretely, in a dramatic and exciting way, by the Bolivarian Revolution in Venezuela. Could we imagine the changes that are occurring here now *without* the power of the state?

And this idea, too, has been refuted *theoretically*—by the understanding of economic systems in general and the conditions for the development of socialism in particular associated with the thought of Karl Marx. For Marx, it was self-evident that workers need the power of the state to create the conditions for a society that could end capitalist exploitation. Similarly, he refused to write detailed models, "recipes" for the society of the future—those "fantastic pictures and plans of a new society" that utopian opponents of capitalism offered. There was a critical reason for both: socialism does not drop from the sky.

Socialism as a Process

No new economic system drops from the sky. Rather than dropping from the sky or emerging pristine and complete from the conceptions of intellectuals, new productive forces and relations of production emerge within and in opposition to the existing society. One implication is that the new society can never be fully formed at the beginning. Initially, that new society must build upon elements of the old society. The socialist society that emerges from capitalism, Marx stressed, is necessarily "economically, morally, and intellectually still stamped with the birthmarks of the old society."

At the core of Marx's dialectical conception is the recognition that a new society comes on the scene necessarily in a defective form and that it develops by transforming its historical premises, by transcending its defects. Only when the new society stands upon its *own* foundations, only when it builds upon premises that it produces *itself*, can we realize the potential that was present in it from the beginning. Marx understood this as a process in which we struggle to liberate ourselves from the burden of the old society.

What exactly was the defect that Marx specifically identified in socialism as it first emerged? Not (as is often expressed) that the productive forces were too low and therefore the principal task would be to develop the productive forces. The particular defect Marx described was the nature of the human beings produced in the old society with the old ideas—people who continue to be self-oriented and therefore consider themselves entitled to get back exactly what they believe they contributed to society. Such a society is characterized by a multitude of exchange transactions—it is one in which everyone calculates in his own self-interest and feels cheated if he does not receive his equivalent. This behavior, Marx was clear, is an inheritance from the old society; it demonstrates clearly that we don't yet think of society as a human family, as one in which liberation of all is the condition for liberation of each.

But this self-orientation would not be the *only* defect present when the new society comes on the scene. The new society is economically, socially, intellectually infected: historic traditions of patriarchy, racism, discrimination, and significant inequalities in education, health, and living standards are among the elements the new society may inherit. Rather than accepting these barriers to human development, however, these defects must be confronted through a process that understands them as defects.

When you recognize that socialism is a process, you understand that the answer to the existence of defects like self-orientation, racism, and patriarchy is not to build institutions that incorporate them. Characteristic of most attempts to build socialism in the twentieth century, for example, was the conclusion that the inherent self-orientation of people means that the most important thing is to provide the necessary economic incentives to induce people to work. Bonus schemes, profit-sharing, various forms of monetary incentives became central; the underlying logic was that the resulting development of productive forces will have a "trickle-down" effect—that the new people will gradually emerge.

In fact, the *opposite* effect occurs. When you try to create the new society by building upon its defects, what it has inherited from the old society, you are *strengthening* the elements of the old society which are inherent in the new society as it initially emerges. When you encourage selfishness, you strengthen a tendency for people to act in their own interests without regard for the interests of others—you reinforce and deepen divisions among individuals, groups, regions, and nations, and you make inequality seem like common sense. When you legitimize the idea that getting more for yourself is in the interests of all, you create the conditions for the return to the old society.

How is it possible to build a new society based upon the principle of self-interest? How can you produce on this basis the people for whom unity based upon recognition of their differences is second nature? Obviously, we cannot *ignore* the nature of the people who emerge from the old society. Precisely because he understood that the subjects of every process are specific human beings, Marx recognized that you could not create *immediately* a society based upon the distribution principle of "to each according to his need." Putting the old subjects into that new structure would inevitably produce disaster. He understood that we cannot go directly to the system of justice and equity appropriate to a true human society, to the human family. However, Marx definitely was not arguing that the way to create the new society was to *build* upon the defects it necessarily contains when it initially emerges.

Rather, the socialist process is a process of both destruction and construction—a process of destroying the remaining elements of the old society (including the support for the logic of capital) and a process of building new, socialist human beings.

Human Beings and Socialism

No one articulated better in the twentieth century the importance of developing new, socialist human beings than Che Guevara. He understood that if you try to build socialism with the help of "the dull instruments left us by capitalism (the commodity as the economic cell, individual material interest as the lever, etc.)," the effect is to undermine the development of consciousness. To build the new society, he stressed, it is necessary, simultaneous with the new material foundations, to build the new man and new woman.

We need to remember the goal. If you don't know where you want to go, then no road will take you there. The world that socialists have always wanted to build is one in which people relate to each other as members of a human family, a society in which we recognize that the welfare of others concerns us; it is a world of human solidarity and love where, in place of classes and class antagonisms, we have "an association, in which the free development of each is the condition for the free development of all."

The world that we want to build is the society of associated producers where each individual is able to develop his full potential—the world which in Marx's view would permit the "absolute workingout of his creative potentialities," the "complete working out of the human content," the "development of all human powers as such the end in itself." The fragmented, crippled human beings that capitalism produces would be replaced by the fully developed human being, "the totally developed individual, for whom the different social functions are different modes of activity he takes up in turn."

But those people don't drop from the sky; there is only one way in which they are produced—through their own activity. Only by exercising both their mental and manual capabilities in every aspect of their lives do human beings develop those capabilities; they produce in themselves specific capacities that allow them to carry out new activities. The simultaneous changing of circumstances and self-change (what Marx called "revolutionary practice") is how we build the new society and new human beings.

Obviously, the nature of our institutions and relations must provide us with the space for such self-development. Without democracy in production, for example, we can build neither a new society nor new people. When workers engage in self-management, they combine the conception of work with its execution. Not only, then, can the intellectual potentialities of *all* the associated producers be developed but the "tacit knowledge" that workers have about better ways to work and produce can also be a social knowledge from which we all benefit. Democratic, participatory, and protagonistic production both draws upon our hidden human resources and develops our capacities. But without that combination of head and hand, people *remain* the fragmented, crippled human beings that capitalism produces: the division between those who *think* and those who *do* continues—as does the pattern that Marx described in which "the development of the human capacities on the one side is based on the restriction of development on the other side." Democracy in production is a necessary condition for the free development of all.

But what is production? It's not something that occurs only in a factory or in what we traditionally identify as a workplace. Every activity with the goal of providing inputs into the development of human beings (especially those which nurture human development directly) must be understood as production. Further, the conceptions that guide production must themselves be produced. The goals that guide production are distinguishing characteristics of societies. In capitalism, they are the goals of the individual capitalist: profits. In a society of associated producers, though, they are the explicit goals for self-development of people in that society. Only through a process in which people are involved in making the decisions that affect them at every relevant level (i.e., their neighborhoods, communities, and society as a whole) can the goals that guide productive activity be the goals of the people themselves. Through their involvement in this democratic decision making, people transform both their circumstances and themselves—they produce themselves as subjects in the new society.

This combination of democratic development of goals and democratic execution of those goals is essential because through it people are able to understand the links between their activities and between themselves. Transparency is the rule in the society of associated producers: it is always clear who has decided what is to be done and how that is being carried out. With transparency the basis of solidarity is strengthened. Understanding our interdependence makes it easier to see our common interests, a unity based upon recognition of our different needs and capacities. We see that our productivity is the result of combining our different capabilities and that our unity and the common ownership of the means of production make us all the beneficiaries of our common efforts. These are the conditions in which all the fruits of cooperation flow abundantly, and we can focus on what is truly important—creation of the conditions in which development of all human powers is the end in itself.

All of these characteristics and relations coexist simultaneously and support one another in the world we want to build. Democratic decision making within the workplace (instead of capitalist direction and supervision), democratic direction by the community of the goals of activity (in place of direction by capitalists), production for the purpose of satisfying needs (rather than for the purpose of exchange), common ownership of the means of production (rather than private or group ownership), a democratic, participatory, and protagonistic form of governance (rather than a state over and above society), solidarity based upon recognition of our common humanity (rather than self-orientation), and the focus upon development of human potential (rather than upon the production of things)—all these are limbs of a new organic system, the truly human society.

So, how can we build this world?

The Process of Socialist Construction

Socialism doesn't drop from the sky. It is necessarily rooted in particular societies. And that is why reliance upon detailed universal models misleads us. (Think about how many left criticisms of the Bolivarian Revolution have their origin in the fact that it differs from the early Soviet Union!) Every society has its unique characteristics—its unique histories, traditions (including religious and indigenous ones), its mythologies, its heroes who have struggled for a better world, and the particular capacities that people have developed in the process of struggle. Since we are talking about a process of human development and not abstract recipes, we understand that we proceed most surely when we choose our own path, one that people recognize as their own (rather than the pale imitation of someone else).

We all start the process of socialist construction, too, from different places in terms of levels of economic development—and that clearly affects how much of our initial activity (if we are dependent upon our own resources) must be devoted to the future. How different, too, are the situations of societies depending on the strength of their domestic capitalist classes and oligarchies, their degree of domination by global capitalist forces, and the extent to which they are able to draw upon the support and solidarity of other societies that have set out on a socialist path.

Further, the historical actors who start us on the way may be quite different in each case: Here a highly organized working-class majority (as in the recipe books of previous centuries); there a peasant army, a vanguard party, a national liberation bloc (electoral or armed), army rebels, an anti-poverty alliance, and variations too numerous to name or yet to emerge. We would be pedantic fools if we insisted that there is only one way to start the social revolution.

However, to construct a socialist society in reality, one step in every particular path is critical—control and transformation of the state. Without the removal of state power from capitalist control, every real threat to capital will be destroyed. The capitalist state is an essential basis of support for the reproduction of capitalist social relations; and the army, police, legal system, and economic resources of the state will be mobilized to stifle every particular inroad that cannot be absorbed. Capital always uses the power of its state when challenged.

In contrast, a state determined to serve as the midwife of a new society can both restrict the conditions for the reproduction of capital and open the door to the elements of the new society. Winning "the battle of democracy" and using "political supremacy to wrest, by degrees, all capital from the bourgeoisie" remains as critical now as when Marx and Engels wrote the *Communist Manifesto*. By ensuring that the means of production come into the possession of the associated producers and are governed increasingly according to their logic and by using state mechanisms to channel resources away from the old and to the new, the workers' state is an essential weapon for carrying out the struggle against capital.

Yet, as Marx knew, this process requires a special kind of state—not the inherited form of state which stands over and above society and is "a public force organized for social enslavement." The state itself must be transformed into one subordinate to society, into the "self-government of the producers." Without creating power from below, rather than the self-development which is at the core of the society of the associated producers, the tendency will be the emergence of a class over and above us—a class that identifies progress with the ability to control and direct from above.

It is important to recognize that Marx did not understand at first that the working class could not use "the ready-made state machinery... for its own purposes." But he learned from history. In particular, he learned that workers in the Paris Commune had spontaneously discovered the necessary form of the workers' state—a democratic and decentralized state from below. "All France," Marx commented, "would have been organized into self-working and self-governing communes." And he responded to the anarchist Bakunin's doubts about the workers' state: Yes, all members of society *would* really be members of government "because the thing starts with self-government of the township." Marx immediately recognized the insight of the workers of Paris because "revolutionary practice" was at the core of his vision.

Revolutionary Practice

For many socialists of the nineteenth century, the way to create the new society was to extract people from capitalism and to demonstrate that a non-capitalist alternative was a superior form of social and economic arrangement; those who argued this often looked to philanthropists or the state to provide the funds for these new demonstration projects. For Marx, such proposals reflected a time when the horrors of capitalism were apparent but not the basis for going beyond capital.

Marx didn't reject the goals of the Utopians. Rather, he argued that "only the means are different and the real conditions of the movement are no longer clouded in utopian fables." And what was the different means that Marx described?: "the militant organization of the working class."

Look to what working people are doing, Marx argued. Through their own struggles to satisfy their needs, they reveal that the battle for a new society is conducted by struggling within capitalism rather than by looking outside. In those struggles workers come to recognize their common interests, they come to understand the necessity to join together against capital. It was not simply the formation of a bloc opposed to capital that emerges out of these struggles. Marx consistently stressed that the very process of struggle was a process of producing people in an altered way; in struggling for their needs, "they acquire a new need—the need for society—and what appears as a means becomes an end." They transform themselves into subjects capable of altering their world.

This is what Marx identified as "revolutionary practice": "the coincidence of the changing of circumstances and human activity or self-change." Marx's message to workers, he noted at one point, was that you have to go through years of struggle "not only in order to bring about a change in society but also to change yourselves." Over twenty years later, he also wrote that workers know that "they will have to pass through long struggles, through a series of historic processes, transforming circumstances and men." In short, the means of achieving that new society were inseparable from the process of struggling for it—only in motion could people rid themselves of "all the muck of ages."

Socialism, for this reason, could never be delivered to people from above. It is the work of the working class itself, Marx argued. That is why the Paris Commune was so important for him. Once we understand that people produce themselves through their own activity, it follows that only where the state as mediator for (and power over) workers gives way to the "self-government of the producers" will there be a continuous process whereby workers can change both circumstances and themselves.

Through a democratic revolution, revolutionary practice permits the self-development of people in all spheres and ensures the conditions for the growth of their capacities. We can judge the progress along that path of socialist construction by the growth in the capacity for self-management by workers, of democratic, participatory, and protagonistic self-government by people in their communities and society as a whole, by the development of real solidarity among people.

When we understand the goal of this process—a society that allows for the full development of human potential—there is a simple question that can be posed of all efforts (regardless of their differing histories and situations): Are the new productive relations being built? The real measure as to whether we are going where we want to go is whether the steps being taken strengthen or weaken the new relation of associated producers. The only true foundation for the new society is the development of self-confidence and unity of the working class, its self-development. Without that, we are building castles in the sand.

Building Socialism of the Twenty-First Century

In the same way that Marx was prepared to change his own views in the light of the Paris Commune, we have to think about socialism now in the light of the experiences of the twentieth century.

We need to understand that socialism of the twenty-first century cannot be a statist society where decisions are top-down and where all initiative is the property of state officeholders or cadres of self-reproducing vanguards. Precisely because socialism focuses upon human development, it stresses the need for a society that is democratic, participatory, and protagonistic. A society dominated by an all-powerful state does not produce the human beings who can create socialism.

For the same reason, socialism is not populism. A society in which people look to the state to provide them with resources and with the answers to all their problems does not foster the development of human capacities; rather, it leaves them as people who look to the state for all answers and to leaders who promise everything.

Further, socialism is not totalitarianism. Precisely because human beings differ and have differing needs and abilities, their development by definition requires recognition and respect for diversity. Neither state nor community pressures for uniformity in productive activity, consumption choices, or lifestyles support the emergence of what Marx welcomed as unity based upon recognition of difference.

We need to recognize, too, that socialism is not the worship of technology — a disease that has plagued Marxism and which in the Soviet Union took the form of immense factories, mines, and collective farms to capture presumed

sumed economies of scale. Rather, we must acknowledge that small enterprises may both permit greater democratic control from below (thus developing the capacities of the producers) and might better preserve an environment that can serve the needs of people.

We can learn the lessons from the experiences of the twentieth century. We know now that the desire to develop a good society for people is not sufficient—you have to be prepared to break with the logic of capital in order to build a better world. And we know now that socialism cannot be achieved from above through the efforts and tutelage of a vanguard that seizes all initiatives and distrusts the self-development of the masses. "The working class," Rosa Luxemburg wisely stressed, "demands the right to make its own mistakes and learn in the dialectic of history." When we begin from the goal of a society that can unleash all the potential of human beings and recognize that the path to that goal is inseparable from the self-development of people, we can build a truly human society.

I suggest, in fact, that many lessons of the twentieth century have been learned and are embodied in the Bolivarian Constitution. In Article 299's emphasis upon "ensuring overall human development"; in the declaration of Article 20 that "everyone has the right to the free development of his or her own personality"; in the focus of Article 102 upon "developing the creative potential of every human being and the full exercise of his or her personality in a democratic society"; in Article 62's declaration that participation by people is "the necessary way of achieving the involvement to ensure their complete development, both individual and collective"; in the identification of democratic planning and participatory budgeting at all levels of society; in Article 70's focus upon "self-management, co-management, cooperatives in all forms" as examples of "forms of association guided by the values of mutual cooperation and solidarity"; and in the obligations, as noted in Article 135, that "by virtue of solidarity, social responsibility, and humanitarian assistance, are incumbent upon private individuals according to their abilities"—the elements of a socialism of the twenty-first century are there in ideal form.

The struggle now is to make them a reality.

6

Seven Difficult Questions

In April 2004, I was invited to make a presentation on the experience of Yugoslav Self-Management to the Commission on the Trade Union Movement in the Bolivarian Revolutionary Process at the Second World Conference of Solidarity with the Bolivarian Revolution in Caracas, Venezuela. In my talk on the lessons from that experience (which was translated and circulated in Venezuela), I identified the basic characteristics of self-management, how it changed over forty years, and some positive and negative aspects.[1]

Within a year, the process of moving toward worker management had accelerated considerably in Venezuela. So, when I was invited to speak at 'Workers in the Revolution: Bolivarian Co-Management, an Alternative Economic Model' in Valencia in April 2005 for the Third World Conference of Solidarity with the Bolivarian Revolution, I decided to focus upon the problems that Venezuelan workers and the Revolution would face in moving toward co-management.

In 2004, in Venezuela the idea of worker management, self-management, co-management, and production by associated producers was basically a demand and a dream. Today, it is being made real—given the steps taken so far at such firms as Invepal, CADAFE, CADELA, and ALCASA (and we hope with more steps to follow soon). That means that you have to prepare yourselves to struggle with the real problems of worker management.

In order to get you to think about these problems, today I want to emphasize the negative side of Yugoslav self-management. In particular, I want to pose what I call seven difficult questions arising from the Yugoslav experience. I think that you need to understand the problems that emerged there. They may appear in some form here (and maybe even in a *worse* form). If they do show up, there will be three possibilities:

1. The problems will not be resolved, and the failure to find good solutions will discredit worker management.
2. They will be solved—by the workers themselves.
3. They will be solved—by someone else.

Before talking about problems, though, let me emphasize that I am convinced that worker management is the only real ultimate alternative to capitalism. When workers cooperate in production and understand that it is not the owners of capital but working people themselves who are the beneficiaries of their activity, worker management can demonstrate that it is a far superior form of organizing productive activity for a number of reasons:

1. Without capitalist exploitation, there is a tendency to cooperate with workers alongside you to do the job well and to take pride in your work rather than trying to do as little as possible.
2. The knowledge workers have in their heads about better ways to do the job, knowledge that is not shared with capitalists, can now be drawn upon to improve production both immediately and for future innovations.
3. You don't need the cost of supervisors and monitors whose main roles are to make certain that the people they watch are working hard. And to the extent that production has been organized not on the basis of efficiency but to make monitoring easier, this and other irrational characteristics of capitalism are no longer necessary.

4. Worker management offers the possibility of combining thinking and doing—of ending the division in the workplace between those who think and those who do. So, it offers the possibility of *all* workers developing their capacities and potential. In this respect, worker management can foster greater productivity and innovation.

Any discussion of problems in Yugoslav self-management must be placed in the proper context: Yugoslavia, it must be remembered today, was once a success story. It was envied as an alternative to both the statist societies of the East and the capitalist societies of the West. There were very high growth rates in the 1950s when self-management was introduced, and although growth declined in the 1960s and 1970s, it remained quite high. Yugoslavia industrialized in this period, moving from a largely peasant agricultural base to a country that exported manufactured goods to Western Europe.

But as I indicated, there were problems. Let me begin with a problem I mentioned in last year's talk—the gap between what workers' councils could do in theory and what they actually did. In 1950, when Marshall Tito introduced the new law on worker self-management, he acknowledged the backwardness of Yugoslav workers and the fears of many that worker control would be premature because "the workers will not be able to master the complicated techniques of management of factories and other enterprises." And Tito's response was—we can't wait for everyone to become educated. "In the very process of management, in the continuous process of work and management, all the workers will gain the necessary experience. They will get acquainted not only with the work process, but also with all the problems of their enterprises. Only through practice will workers be able to learn how to keep records, how much material they may use, and how much they can save.... They will learn how high the accumulation of their enterprise has to be... and how much of the remainder of the surplus product can be used to raise their standard of living."

Now, as I indicated last time, Yugoslav workers actually did become well informed about their enterprises, and many had experience in serving on workers councils at the shop and enterprise levels. However, something that

Tito assumed would happen did *not* occur. In 1975, twenty-five years after the new law was introduced, a Yugoslav writer, Jose Goricar, described the gap between workers and the managers and their experts this way:

> It appears either as a functional differentiation, a hierarchy of knowledge and expertise, or as a consequence of atomized and monotonous industrial operations that offer the worker… only meager opportunity for developing, in performing his duties, any substantial measure of freedom of thought, imagination, and inventiveness. If we add to all this the comparatively long and tiring working day, we have the complete set of circumstances that fetter the workers from engaging more intensively in the management of their work organizations.[2]

What had happened? Although the members of the workers' councils had the *power* to decide on critical questions like investments, marketing, and production decisions, they didn't feel they had the competence to make these decisions—compared with the managers and technical experts. So in many enterprises, the workers' councils tended to rubber-stamp the proposals that came from management. (After all, the managers shared in the income of the firm and had a common interest in the firm doing well.) The workers' councils spent a lot of time discussing things that they did feel competent to judge—like the fairness of relative incomes within the enterprise. And when they went to blame the managers over results that didn't turn out well, the managers responded—*you* made the decision. However, that wasn't an answer that workers accepted; often, the position they took was, we do our work well, and we expect *you* to do your work well. And the workers' councils occasionally removed managers who had made bad proposals. In such cases, they functioned like an electorate unhappy with its government, but not as the government themselves.

How can you avoid this situation, this gap between experts and workers? Twenty-five years after the introduction of worker management, it was still there. Goricar said it was the low level of development and that workers needed to self-instruct and self-educate themselves. But in pointing to the monotonous and long, tiring working days, he himself reveals the problem in any suggestion that workers educate themselves.

Let me suggest that the basic problem was that there was no education occurring in the workplace. Why wasn't learning the principles of accounting, book-keeping, marketing, etc., all part of the job? Not something to be added on to a long, tiring workday—but rather something to be *incorporated* into the workday. In other words, a redefinition of work to include the process of producing the workers that worker management needs.

Obviously, this involves the expansion of the nontraditional workday and the shortening of the traditional workday (for which increased productivity and efficiency is essential). This was not something that Yugoslav self-managed enterprises did. The result? In many enterprises, workers had the power legally but weren't able to use it.

Redefining work and the workday to include learning is just one possible solution to this problem. The question you have to think about is how to make self-management realize its potential.

The first question I want to pose, then, is: *How do we break down this division within the enterprise between those who think and those who do?*

Let me turn now to a series of problems related to the way Yugoslav self-managed enterprises functioned in the economy. What happened, for example, when demand for the products they produced fell? We know what happens in capitalism: if profits can't be made by selling commodities, people are laid off, put out of work. That didn't happen in the Yugoslav enterprises. There was solidarity among the workers in each enterprise—how could you put members of your collective out of work?

So, the enterprises continued producing—even without sales, they produced for inventory. In terms of the stability of the economy as a whole, compared to capitalism that's not bad, because incomes are maintained and a recession will not be deepened as the result of unemployment. However, not only did the enterprises pay the workers their personal incomes but they also needed to purchase raw materials. So how did they do this without running into serious financial difficulties? Well, they turned to the banks to borrow funds to get them through these periods. And the banks (which were

often partnerships between large self-managed enterprises and local governments) tended to lend in these cases. However, it did raise the problem of
the dependence of firms on the banks and also, as the result of liberal bank
policies, was a source of inflationary tendencies.

Those were problems. But what were the solutions? The second question, then, is: *What should be done in a worker-managed enterprise when
sales fall?*

Let me expand on this by pointing to another characteristic of Yugoslav
self-management. There was solidarity among workers within single enterprises but not between workers in different, competing enterprises. Che
Guevara commented in 1959 after visiting Yugoslavia that we shouldn't lose
sight of the fact that the profits of these enterprises were divided among the
workers; however, each firm, he noted, was "engaged in violent struggle with
its competitors over prices and quality." Che also observed that there was a
real danger there, because this competition could "introduce factors that
distort what the socialist spirit should presumably be."[3]

Yes, there definitely was a lack of solidarity between workers in competing enterprises. But that wasn't the only problem. There was also duplica-
tion of investment. These enterprises were struggling to serve the same market and investing for that purpose. One result was a tendency for excess
capacity in many sectors (especially in the 1970s and 1980s). That made
enterprises more vulnerable financially and more dependent on the banks.
Thus, a third question: *What should be the role in worker management of
competition between workers in different enterprises?*

Now the solidarity among workers within a particular enterprise had
another side. What workers in Yugoslavia wanted to do was to increase
income per worker in their enterprises (both immediately and in the longer
term), so their tendency was to invest in the most modern, machine-intensive
technology. This had a very good effect—it led to significant productivity
increases. The negative side of it, however, was that investments of this kind
did not generate many new jobs. Thus when people moved from the countryside into the cities in search of higher incomes, they didn't find jobs; the
result was unemployment or migration as guest workers to Western Europe.

In the 1950s, this problem of generating new jobs was resolved by the state taxing the enterprises and using those resources to create new self-managed enterprises. But this was something that made workers in the existing enterprises unhappy—they argued that state taxation was preventing them from making the investments *they* needed to make. How could you say there was self-management, they argued, when workers couldn't control the income they were creating? How could workers really rule if a Stalinist state was exploiting the enterprises and making the important decisions? In the 1960s, the role of the federal state was substantially reduced: state taxation of enterprises fell, the role of the state in investments dropped, and unemployment rose.

This brings us to a fourth question: *What responsibility do workers in self-managed enterprises have for the unemployed and the excluded? Who is responsible for creating jobs?*

Besides the unemployment that emerged in the 1960s, there was also growing inequality between enterprises and thus between workers in different enterprises. It wasn't necessarily because workers in rich enterprises deserved it. You could be doing precisely the same thing in two enterprises and receive substantially higher income in one enterprise than in the other simply because of the industry you were lucky enough to be in, or because monopolies or other market factors favored your enterprise. There was a saying in Yugoslavia: "It's not what you do, it's where you do it." Workers in poorer enterprises didn't think that was fair, and they tended to look with envy at the rising incomes of workers in the richer enterprises. Accordingly, they responded by distributing more of their firm's earnings in the form of personal income. To make the investments that would keep them competitive and increase their future income, they had to turn to the banks; that is, the poorer enterprises became more dependent upon banks.

But remember, the richer enterprises often were part owners of the banks. When I began to study Yugoslav self-management, one of the things I wondered about was whether their relations to the banks created any problems between rich and poor enterprises. I met with a member of the Central Committee of the League of Communists in 1978, and I asked him,

"Isn't it possible that rich firms can use their influence in the banks to pressure poor firms that need credit?" And he answered, "Yes, it's terrible! We know of cases where poorer firms are pressured to sell at low prices to the richer firms in order to get any credit from the banks!" (Now, remember, these were not capitalist firms—these were self-managed enterprises in which the workers got the income.) Well, I was shocked. It was far worse than I feared. So, I asked him, "What do you do about this?" (And by "you," I meant the League of Communists of Yugoslavia.) He answered, "We tell them that this is not in the interests of the working class as a whole. We try to convince them not to do this type of thing. But," he continued, "we don't hit them on the head—that is not our role." He and I then had an interesting discussion about Antonio Gramsci and the idea of the party as organic intellectual.

But *there* was the problem: the individual enterprises were obviously not acting in the interests of the working class as a whole, the state *could* not act in the interests of the working class as a whole, and the party *would* not. The result is that inequality grew between enterprises and between republics and, under the slogan of self-management, privilege grew for specific groups of workers and solidarity fell.

So, here is question five: *In a system of worker self-management, who looks after the interests of the working class as a whole?*

This is definitely one of the most fundamental questions. But let me add another related to the problems of self-management in Yugoslavia. As I indicated, a situation that emerged was that the weaker enterprises became dependent upon banks. In some cases, they were turning to banks not only to borrow money for the purpose of making investments but also to provide personal income for members of their collectives. This was entirely contrary to the theory of socialist commodity production, which stated that the personal income of workers should come from the sales made by their enterprises. But sitting among the directors of the banks would be not only representatives of the self-managed enterprises who were owners but were also representatives of local government, the commune. And the representative of the commune would say, "*Give* them the money. Give them the money because if you don't, the enterprise will fail and it will be the commune that will be responsible for looking after the workers."

In other words, there were reasons why firms were kept alive—to avoid the problem of unemployment and the dislocation when a firm goes bankrupt. But this produces something that economists call the problem of the "soft budget constraint": the argument is that if a firm knows it will be rescued, it doesn't need to take the actions necessary to solve its problems. For example, rather than increasing its efficiency or dropping product lines that weaken it, the firm may spend a lot of time making certain it has friends in high places who will keep it alive. How rational is that for the economy? In the Yugoslav case, they tried to resolve the problem by merging weak firms with stronger firms, which led to rationalization and reorganization of the weaker firms without generating unemployment, but the growth of large and complex firms did raise the question of whether worker influence was being reduced in the process.

All this points to a sixth question: *Should worker-managed enterprises be allowed to fail?*

Consider the experience in Yugoslavia. Acting in their own self-interest, workers in individual enterprises in Yugoslavia were successful in demonstrating that capitalists are not necessary, that workers' councils can direct managers and technical staff to make decisions in their interest and that these enterprises will tend to introduce new technology that increases productivity and income per worker. That was one of the most important lessons in Yugoslavia, and it is one of the most important things to demonstrate here.

But Yugoslavia also demonstrated that self interest within individual enterprises is not enough. Not only does the Yugoslav experience demonstrate that solidarity within a particular enterprise does not necessarily mean solidarity within the society, it also indicates that the failure to resolve problems in this relationship can put real limits on the development of worker management. Even the links they attempted to create between workers in different enterprises, between workers in commodity-producing sectors and those in the social sector, between producers and communities were dominated by one issue: self-interest. What was missing was a sense of solidarity within the society.

The result was unemployment, growing inequality, envy, inflationary tendencies, rising social and ethnic tensions—and ultimately, the inability to unite against forces outside the country. The failure to foster solidarity within the society left it vulnerable to the pressures of finance capital and imperialist intervention. Yugoslavia had unique characteristics of ethnic and religious differences and a vast gap between the economic levels of differing republics; however, when differences are not dissolved in a process of building solidarity, they are there to be exploited.

Think about the questions I've posed so far:

1. How do we break down the division within the enterprise between those who think and those who do?
2. What should be done in a worker-managed enterprise when sales fall?
3. What should be the role in worker management of competition between workers in different enterprises?
4. What responsibility do workers in self-managed enterprises have for the unemployed and the excluded?
5. In a system of worker self-management, who looks after the interests of the working class as a whole?
6. Should worker-managed enterprises be allowed to fail?

With the exception of the first question, concerning the gap between experts and workers, all of these questions are variations on a particular theme: What is the relation between an individual worker-managed enterprise and society as a whole? That is, they are questions that start from the premise that there is a separation between the worker-managed enterprise and the rest of society. Unfortunately, in a society in which roughly 50 percent of the working class is in the informal sector and estimates of poverty range up to 80 percent of the population, the premise of a division between an aristocracy of labor in specific enterprises and the majority of the working class is not unthinkable. Nor should we forget the problems that such a division can generate.

If we *don't* begin from the premise of a separation between the worker-managed enterprises and the rest of society, however, then many of these difficult questions look quite different. For example, if the sales of a worker-managed enterprise fall, *obviously* it shouldn't continue producing things for which there is no demand—but there must be many products that the enterprise *can* produce at that time that the community needs, and there must be many needs of the local communities to which the workers can turn their attention instead of working in the specific enterprise. Similarly, why should workers in any particular enterprises have any greater responsibility for the unemployed than society as a whole? And shouldn't the interests of the working class as a whole be the concern of all workers?

The critical question, in short, is how to avoid a problem that characterized self-management in Yugoslavia—the lack of solidarity within the working class as a whole. Of course, the State can take on the responsibility of taxing worker-managed enterprises and using the resources to generate employment and reduce poverty. However, the Yugoslav example demonstrates that if workers believe that they and they alone are entitled to the incomes secured by their enterprises, it is not difficult for them to view the State as distant, inefficient, and exploitative.

And that brings us to our seventh question: *How can solidarity between worker-managed enterprises and society as a whole be incorporated directly into those enterprises?*

Is it possible for workers to incorporate into their discussions consideration of the needs of their communities—not only their immediate communities but also more distant, relatively disadvantaged communities? Clearly, development in this direction is a process. And it is the process envisioned in the Bolivarian constitution. As Article 135 stresses, there is not simply the obligation of the State to the general welfare of society, there are also "the obligations which, by virtue of solidarity, social responsibility, and humanitarian assistance, are incumbent upon private individuals according to their abilities."

With its idea of linking the needs of communities, expressed through democratic local planning, to the capabilities of self-managing producers, the constitution envisions an alternative economic model—one marked by concepts of justice, equality, solidarity, democracy, and social responsibility. Guided by those ideals of the constitution, I suggest that you can avoid many of the problems that plagued the Yugoslav model—particularly those that resulted from their focus on self-interest rather than the interests of the working class as a whole.

7

The Revolution of Radical Needs:
Behind the Bolivarian Choice of a Socialist Path

Only a revolution of radical needs can be a radical revolution....To be radical is to grasp the root of the matter. But, for man, the root is man himself.
—Karl Marx

A spectre is haunting capitalism.[1] Behind growing attacks on capitalist globalization and neoliberal economic policies, there is the hint that something is dying—something more than particular forms of capitalism, something more than the current distribution of power and domination (which governments in service of local elites, capitalists, and oligarchies would like to modify ... just a bit).

There are, of course, the morbid symptoms—the sanctimonious aggression of "the greatest nation" that ever bombed the earth, the tears of melting ice shed by a natural world stripped and strip-mined in the drive for profit, the race to abandon commitments to workers and workers themselves, the race to the bottom that is barbarism.

Something else, though, can be glimpsed. A challenge to capital that starts from the needs of human beings. An assertion that what really matters is not that the worker exist to satisfy capital's drive for growth but "the inverse situation, in which objective wealth is there to satisfy the worker's own need for development."[2] Human development, the growth of human capabilities, the expansion of human capacities—today, an alternative "ought" to that of capital, begins to present itself, the ought of a better world. Today, Marx's conception of "the rich human being," that "rich individuality which is as all-sided in its production as in its consumption" has begun to emerge from the shadows to which it had been banished in the twentieth century.[3]

The Cunning of History: A Venezuelan Story

And, typical of the surprises, the chequered and devious course, that history always offers, this spectre has appeared at a most unpredictable site—Venezuela.[4] Not that the enormous gulf between the ostentatious wealth and consumerism of a rent-capturing minority, on the one side, and the overwhelming poverty of the vast majority on the other makes Venezuela an unlikely place to say "no" to the status quo. But, offering a real (rather than rhetorical) "yes" to a new logic of human development demands more than a scream of protest; it requires a vision, the means to satisfy needs, and power. And, all this and more is needed if this is to be a site where "socialism for the twenty-first century" can be constructed.

Could that be anticipated in a country where oil rents had not only enriched a minority but also contributed to the virtual disappearance of manufacturing and agriculture (and, thus, of the industrial working class and peasantry, the chosen people of twentieth-century socialism)? Where the combination of oil-driven exchange rates and transnational corporation restructuring squelched non-oil exports and smothered domestic production with cheap imports? Where a stampede of peasants into the cities—encouraged by land monopolization, inadequate interior infrastructure, and higher urban incomes—produced the raw material for a working class over 50 percent in the informal sector? An oil economy in which a large portion of the population, in formal and informal sectors, sells goods produced outside the country to one another. An oil economy where parts of the country are at the level of centuries ago—lacking electricity, running water, paved roads—and estimates of poverty range up to 80 percent. Socialism for the twenty-first century in Venezuela?

Oil wealth, too, has done far more than simply warp the Venezuelan economy. To the extent that the state has been able to capture international income in the form of oil rents, it has stood over and above Venezuelan society rather than rested upon it. As the recipient of rent (and source of the same for the underlying population), the state itself became the supreme object of desire. Local production of value was subordinated to the capture of rent: "In Venezuela class struggle centered on the state, with the primary focus not on the appropriation of domestically produced surplus value but on the capture of state-mediated oil rents." [5] A parasitic capitalist class and a pervasive culture of clientelism and corruption are the natural offspring of rent-seeking behavior raised to such commanding heights.

Here was a culture, it was said, in which prizes were awarded for those who could steal the most from the state, where "just put me where the money is" was the refrain for real men. Since the money was in the state, control of the state—a matter too important to be left to the masses—was essential; to this end, the "democratic parties" fashioned a pact to ensure that state power, jobs, and money would remain in safe hands (i.e., theirs). And, the impoverished majority, the "demos"? Some manna from above in good times; neglect, always.

"Every minute hundreds of children are born in Venezuela, whose health is endangered for lack of food and medicine, while billions are stolen from the national wealth, and in the end what remains of the country is bled dry," wrote Hugo Chávez Frias from jail in 1993. Chávez, a military officer imprisoned for leading a rebellion in 1992 against the regime of "alienating political lies" that was enslaving the Venezuelan people "in the name of democracy," declared that "there's no reason why one should give any credence to a political class that demonstrated toward society that it has no will at all to institute change."[6]

A warped economy with parasitic capitalists, a culture of corruption and clientalism, a sham democracy (naturally approved by the imperialist colossus to the north)—so foul a sky clears not without a storm. And a storm is what Venezuela has needed. More than one. An economic revolution, a political revolution, a cultural revolution.

Neoliberalism and Its Discontents

Although there was much talk in the 1970s about "sowing the oil" (i.e., using the high state revenues in this period of high oil prices to transform Venezuela into a modern industrial economy), high state expenditures and schemes had little effect. Venezuela remained an oil exporter and little else. So, when oil prices crashed in the 1980s (and did so without a corresponding retrenchment of the pattern of high consumption imports and high state spending built upon high oil revenues), Venezuela found itself with massive twin deficits in trade and budgets. Its international reserves depleted, the Venezuelan government yielded to the demands of international capital and introduced a policy of neoliberalism.

It is well-known that the Venezuelan masses responded in 1989 with a loud "No!" to the price increases that were the first instalment in the neoliberal package. As often occurs, though, this spontaneous eruption, the "Caracazo," while full of sound and fury, ultimately signified very little. Neoliberalism proceeded in the 1990s with a pattern of privatizations and cutbacks, and the nationalized oil company PDVSA performed the magical trick of causing state oil revenues to disappear (through transfer pricing) while welcoming back transnational oil companies into Venezuelan oil fields.

Indeed, the only lasting effect of the Caracazo was the military revolt of 1992 that its brutal suppression stimulated. Not because the rebellion itself succeeded but because its leader, Hugo Chávez, emerged as a popular hero, rejecting neoliberalism and pledging to bring a real democracy to Venezuela, one that went far beyond parliamentary democracy. Rather than putting the Venezuelan people asleep in order to enslave them by making the act of voting "into the beginning and end of democracy," Chávez wrote in 1993 that "the sovereign people must transform itself into the object *and the subject* of power. This option is not negotiable for revolutionaries."[7]

Opening the Battle of Democracy

Chávez was elected president in 1998 and immediately called for a Constituent Assembly to rewrite the constitution of Venezuela. By 2000, Venezuela had a new name (the Bolivarian Republic of Venezuela), a new constitution (the Bolivarian Constitution), and a new National Assembly and president elected under that constitution.

Here was a constitution that returns over and over again to the theme of human development as the goal, which stresses the importance of dignity and solidarity for the realization of human potential and embodies the concept of a human family—one whose relations are based upon "equality of rights and duties, solidarity, common effort, mutual understanding, and reciprocal respect." The view is one of a society where "obligations which, by virtue of solidarity, social responsibility, and humanitarian assistance, are incumbent upon private individuals according to their abilities."

Here, too, was a vision of new Bolivarian subjects producing themselves — both in the political sphere ("the participation of the people in forming, carrying out and controlling the management of public affairs is the necessary way of achieving the involvement to ensure their complete development, both individual and collective") and in the economic sphere ("self-management, co-management, cooperatives in all forms, including those of a financial nature, savings funds, community enterprises, and other forms of association guided by the values of mutual cooperation and solidarity"). This is a constitution that demands a "democratic, participatory, and protagonistic" society, a constitution whose premise is that the full development of human beings as subjects is based upon their "active, conscious, and joint participation in the processes of social transformation embodied in the values which are part of the national identity."

This is not the language of capital—nor its logic. Throughout the constitution is this thread of the logic of human needs, activity, and development. So, was this an anti-capitalist constitution? A constitution for socialism of the twenty-first century?

Not quite. While the Bolivarian constitution says nothing about capitalism as such, it does contain within it key elements supportive of capitalism: it guarantees the right of property (Article 115), identifies a role for private initiative in generating growth and employment (Article 299), calls upon the state to promote private initiative (Article 112), entrenches in the constitution the requirement for a balanced budget (on a multiyear budget basis), and provides for autonomy for the Venezuelan Central Bank in formulating and implementing monetary policy (Articles 311 and 318).

So, a constitution quite supportive of capitalism (and, indeed, elements of the neoliberal "Washington Consensus") and, on the other hand, containing a subversive element (the focus on human development and a "democratic, participatory and protagonistic society") in which the people are to be "the object *and the subject* of power." Should we be surprised, though, at the coexistence of two seemingly incompatible tendencies in this document?

On the contrary, we should recognize that the Bolivarian constitution represented a snapshot of the balance of forces at the time. In this respect, it could contain contradictory or incompatible elements—support for the logic of capital, on the one hand, and the subversive focus upon human development and revolutionary practice on the other. Although this particular combination was consistent with Chávez's own initial belief that a third way between capitalism and socialism was possible, the ultimate question was—and remains—which element would win.

Directing the Economy

If we look at the initial direction of the economy, as set out in the National Plan of Development for 2001–2007, the dominant tendency was clear. Venezuela needed to diversify its economy; it needed to achieve an economic balance, moving away from the overwhelming reliance upon oil and propelling the development of sectors such as agriculture and industry to serve both local and international markets. And, the Plan proposed that this be achieved by relying upon private initiative and investment, with the presence of the state in strategic industries. To this was to be added the development of the "social economy," an "alternative and complementary road" to the private sector and the public sector, one composed of family, cooperative, and self-managed micro-enterprises.

The conception of the economy here certainly differed from the neoliberal model. The Plan rejected the neoliberal worship of the market, rejected privatization of oil and other state industries, and was determined to use the state actively. But, it was not a rejection of capitalism.

Indeed, one striking aspect was how *little* a role was conceived for the self-managing and cooperative activities by which the "complete development, both individual and collective" of people was to be achieved. The units of the social economy envisioned were small—they were to be encouraged through the democratization of capital, training, and micro-financing from institutions such as the Women's Development Bank. By reducing regulations and tax burdens (a familiar neoliberal solution) and providing training, the informal sector could be incorporated into the social economy; it is necessary, the Plan argued, "to transform the informal workers into small managers." The goal of the state here was acknowledged as that of "creating an emergent managerial class."

But, the social economy was not at the core of the Plan. The real focus of the proposal to transform the economy was to encourage private capital—both domestic and foreign. The state needed to create more favorable conditions for investment: developing financial stability, encouraging the creation of production chains for the fabrication of natural resources, establishing free trade zones, promoting the stock market "to create a growing democratization of managerial capitalism," stabilizing exchange rates, and generally developing an "atmosphere of trust for foreign-owned investment in the country."

An alternative to neoliberalism—but definitely not an anti-capitalist alternative. This is quite clear from the theoretical conception that inspired this alternative: Osvaldo Sunkel's *Development from Within: Toward a Neostructuralist Approach for Latin America*, a collective work by Latin American economists. Neostructuralism, Sunkel explained, "emerged as a theoretical alternative to orthodox neoconservative adjustment programs," identifying the primary sources of Latin American underdevelopment as "endogenous structural factors."[8] Precisely because these problems were deep-rooted, going far beyond solution by marginal adjustments, the state was needed to play an active and dynamic role.

But this was not to be done by looking *inward*, "replacing previously imported goods with locally produced goods" (as earlier structuralists had stressed). For one, that strategy had "failed to generate a modern and competitive national entrepreneurial class."[9] Rather, the orientation of the state in the new structuralism would be to create a basis for development *from within* by mobilizing internal resources and removing obstacles to their efficient combination. In this strategy for "endogenous development," the active state would work the supply side—not as entrepreneur but as facilitator, correcting market failures and encouraging the development of technology, productivity growth, and accumulation.

Here was an industrial strategy that Sunkel proposed begins "by establishing those industries considered to be the essential pillars for creating what we would call today a basic endogenous nucleus for industrialization, accumulation, the generation and diffusion of technical progress, and the increase of productivity."[10] The goal would be to acquire "dynamic comparative advantages" that would allow national sectors not only to serve the local market but also to pursue "new forms of insertion into a difficult but not impenetrable international context."

Certainly, this was a rejection of neoliberalism. However, while Sunkel and his colleagues took pains to stress continuity with the original structuralist arguments, there was a concrete example underlying much of their approach—the balancing of a development strategy and the market by the state in the East Asian experiences. The neostructuralists looked to the use of the state in Japan and South Korea for the assimilation of technology and the coordination of decision making—indeed, for the creation of an "endogenous mechanism of accumulation and generation of technical progress"—as the alternative to neoliberalism for Latin America. The book concluded by noting that the balance of state and market proposed by Latin American neostructuralism "can appropriately be described as a "government-assisted, free market strategy."[11]

It would be difficult to overestimate the importance of the Sunkel book in developing the economic policy orientation of the new Venezuelan government. The constant focus upon "endogenous development" in Venezuela originates here: Chávez had read the book while in prison and has continued to call for it to be read in schools, ministries, and enterprises—precisely because of the radical rupture it represents with the neoliberal model. Development from within, he stresses, builds upon potential from within.

However, while the East Asian examples of endogenous development drew upon strong capitalist conglomerates (the keiretsu, chaebols, etc.,) with which the state could interact, Venezuela had a parasitic, rent-seeking capitalist class. The potential for development from within and the elements that could be mobilized (and indeed *should* be mobilized) was clearly different.

Establishing the Preconditions for Change

The Bolivarian Republic of Venezuela had a new constitution by 1999, but that is not the same as changing reality. There still was the immense poverty, the unemployment and disguised unemployment in the informal sector (much of which is simply the reserve army of labor), and the accumulated social debt. Now the masses of exploited and excluded had hopes and expectations—stimulated by that constitution which promised dignity, social justice, and a protagonistic democracy in which the masses would be the subject of power.

But a precondition for fulfilling those expectations was that laws embodying the constitution's goals had to be passed and that the money for programs (both economic and social) had to be available. The government had begun to make some changes—establishing institutions such as the

Women's Development Bank to support the development of the social economy, mobilizing the military (through Plan Bolivar) to provide social programs and support for the poor, and shifting funds to education in order to
increase the number of children in schools. There were, however, limits to
the funds available—despite Venezuela's oil wealth.

For one, oil prices had plummeted as the result, in large part, of the
flouting of OPEC quotas (a process in which PDVSA, Venezuela's nationalized oil company, had taken the lead). Further, PDVSA—determined that
oil revenues properly belonged to it and not to the Venezuelan state to
squander—succeeded in squirreling away its revenues where they were out
of reach. Thus, the Chávez government was immediately pitted against the
"state" both on the need to strengthen OPEC (which went counter to the
PDVSA management policy of maximizing volume and to the International
Energy Agency, the organization of oil-consuming countries), and also on
the need to alter the relationship between the state and PDVSA in relation
to oil revenues.

The first of these battles was relatively easily won: through state visits to
OPEC countries, Chávez spearheaded the strengthening of OPEC and thus
oil prices. The latter, though, required new laws (and doing something
about long-term agreements made with foreign oil companies). A new law
reestablishing royalties on oil, the hydrocarbon tax, would become one of
the controversial 49 laws proclaimed by Chávez in November 2001.
Although this law affected only new oil production, it clearly demonstrated
the new direction of the government.

In November 2000, with the difficulties in getting legislation through the
National Assembly apparent, Chávez received the approval (given before to
him and preceding presidents) to enact laws of empowerment in specified
areas within one year. And, so, in November 2001, the 49 Laws—including
laws in relation to cooperatives, microfinance, land reform, fisheries, and
oil—were proclaimed. And, the opposition—led by capital—immediately
escalated their attacks on the government.

But what specifically was capital rejecting? Considered one by one,
these laws definitely were not socialist measures as opposed to attempts to

reform Venezuelan capitalism. Measures to support cooperatives, provide for microfinance, and obtain greater revenues for the state from oil—these were not attacks on capitalism. Even the law expropriating idle land from lat-ifundia for the purpose of distributing it to peasants was not a rejection of capitalism as such (as opposed to "feudalism").

Capitalism in Venezuela could have absorbed these reforms, which could have brought more stability to an unstable society. But the whole is greater than the sum of its parts taken separately. As a package, these new laws—oriented toward meeting human needs and integrated through this specific ideology—*were* an attack on capital as such. And capital grasped this. Both local capitalists and imperialism, with its particular interest in the continued domination of finance capital and the previous trajectory toward privatization of the oil industry, understood that this articulated package of reforms represented the assertion (implicit and explicit) of an alternative rather than mere isolated changes.

And so, too, did the Bolivarian Circles, the organizations of supporters that Chávez called for in June and swore in during the month of December 2001. Both sides grasped the significance of the 49 Laws better than assort-ed leftists with their revolutionary checklists who could see only a series of measures characteristic of bourgeois reforms. The package organized both opponents and supporters of the government.

Thus, when the oligarchy, with the active support of imperialism, pro-ceeded to remove Chávez through a coup in April 2002, the masses had a basic organization that could mobilize them. Two days after it began, the coup was reversed as the result of that mobilization and of a military that overwhelmingly supported the Bolivarian Constitution.

The Sword in the Hand of the Social Revolution

"Sporadic slaveholders' insurrections" interrupt the work of peaceful progress, but, Marx commented, they "only accelerate the movement, by putting the sword into the hand of the Social Revolution."[12]

But the crushing of the April coup did *not* put the sword in the hand of the Bolivarian Revolution. On the contrary, Chávez—uncertain of how deep his support was, especially within the military—proceeded very cautiously. He replaced his economic ministers with people who were seen as acceptable to capital and brought back as president of PDVSA a person seen as a consensus candidate. Capital retained all its positions of power— its overwhelming influence in the mass media, its strength in certain sectors such as food processing and distribution, its organizational arm of Fedecamaras (and its partner, the CTV, the opposition party–dominated labor federation), as well as its all-important allies in control of PDVSA management.

This was not, however, a situation that could continue. Not if the promises made to now-awakened masses were to be satisfied. That was not possible without a reversal in the policies followed by existing oil management. Further, the opposition, which retained all its economic power, had not succeeded in its goal of getting rid of Chávez and reversing the new policies adopted. So, the situation was inherently unstable. After continued agitation, capital moved again in early December to bring the government down through a general lockout (supported by its client labor federation). This time the attack centered on the oil company; the goal was to cut off all government revenue, and the expectation was that Chávez would be out by Christmas.

However, as in April, capital completely underestimated the support of the people and the army for the Bolivarian Revolution and its promises. Despite the abandonment of the industry and direct sabotage by the technicians of the oil company, the production workers, joined by retired technicians and support from the army, kept the oil flowing. The general lockout introduced by capital drove the government to take actions to survive; in the face, for example, of the shutdown of stores, the government used the military to introduce its own source of supply of foodstuffs by importing and creating new distribution channels. Throughout, people organized from below—reopening shutdown schools, distributing gasoline, and defending gas stations.

In this process new actors emerged—the Positive Middle Class and the organized working class. Not only the workers in the oil industry who kept PDVSA running but also trade unions in several sectors (steel, subway workers, etc.), who refused to go along with the lockout, rejected the position of the CTV and created thereby the basis for a new labor federation. With the shutdowns of many firms, there were worker takeovers (e.g., in the Sheraton Hotel in the state of Vargas) which kept the firms operating.

Despite great privation, enormous damage to the economy, not least of which was the sabotaged oil industry, and general turmoil, capital's lockout was defeated after several months. This was not like the few days of the April coup. These were *months* of daily struggle, and this battle was won by the masses, who were prepared to struggle to support what they saw as *their* government and who transformed themselves in the course of transforming circumstances.

The slaveholders' revolt had put the sword in the hands of the masses. And, this time the government responded without any efforts at conciliation. Eighteen thousand PDVSA managers and technical staff who had tried to bring down the government—about 40 percent of the entire PDVSA payroll—were fired. The state within the state was dissolved. Venezuelan capital had used its main weapon, the capital strike, and lost it; with that, the economic threat was defused. In April 2003, the government celebrated the first anniversary of the coup and its reversal with an international solidarity meeting. Immediately after, Chávez reinstalled as planning minister Jorge Giordani (who had been removed after the coup) and announced, "We resume the offensive."

Now, as state revenues began to improve in the remainder of 2003, the government proceeded along a path that was implicit in a constitution oriented toward the development of human potential: it took the money from oil and "sowed" it in the basic prerequisites for human development—education and health. Barrio Adentro, the program bringing Cuban doctors into the poorest neighborhoods, began in April 2003 and was extended to the country as a whole six months later. Mission Robinson, the basic literacy program, began in July and was followed by a host of other education programs (so much so that it could be said a year later that half the population was involved in education programs). And Mission Mercal, building upon the government distribution of food during the general lockout, was established in early 2004, bringing significantly subsidized food to the poor.

While these programs began the critical process of tackling the social debt that had been inherited (and would prove absolutely crucial in cementing the support Chávez received from the poor in the August 2004 recall referendum), they were only a beginning. Because the question remained— how were people to survive? What kind of jobs would be available for the currently exploited and excluded as they emerged from the education programs? And what would be the relation to the direction outlined in the 2001–2007 National Plan?

Radical Endogenous Development

No realistic discussion of a desirable development path for Venezuela (capitalist, third way, or socialist of any variety) is possible unless we begin with the real needs of Venezuelans. The basic needs of the majority for food, health care, education, housing, and infrastructure to support that housing are overwhelming. The satisfaction of those needs is, in large part, the measure by which Venezuelans will judge the Bolivarian Revolution. Capitalism failed them; however, the "neostructuralist" alternative as outlined by Sunkel and his colleagues was not a solution for Venezuelan development.

Not only did Venezuela lack Japan's and South Korea's particular capitalist institutions, but it also lacked their relative income equality as the result of land reform and investments in education. Rather, Venezuela had poverty, a vast informal sector, and a huge social debt. Further, it had one very significant "inward-looking" requirement: as a country that had come to import 70 percent of its food requirements, the Bolivarian Revolution was committed to develop "food sovereignty," to "guarantee the population a secure food supply" (in the words of the constitution), and to provide the institutions, infrastructure, training, and technical assistance necessary both to develop food production and to promote rural development.

Development from within, development that originates from the inside, though, *was* an appropriate approach for Venezuela. However, Venezuela's specific needs and conditions meant that it would have to *invent* rather than copy, that it would have to develop its own conception of endogenous development.

The focus on endogenous development began on a relatively modest scale, given the limited resources initially available. Nuclei of Endogenous Development, integrating new projects in particular zones where they could receive technical and financial advice, was a program for sustainable agrarian development rooted in local communities. Support for these new projects and development of the concept of the social economy by the Ministry for the Social Economy (later divided into the Bank of Economic and Social Development and a new Ministry for the Popular Economy) were initial steps in this process.

In March 2004, a much more ambitious program was launched, Mission Vuelvan Caras ('Turn Your Faces). The immediate problem the government faced was what was to be done with the excluded as they came out of the various education missions. Clearly, their expectations would be raised. How could the growing confidence and sense of dignity they felt be nurtured rather than disappointed? Propelled by the minister of labor, Maria Cristina Iglesias, Vuelvan Caras began by recruiting one million people within the missions for the new program. But, explicitly, this was not intended as an employment program—it was much more. Rather, the goal was to begin to transform Venezuela economically, politically, and culturally through a focus upon endogenous development.

Given the immediate needs of the country, Vuelvan Caras stressed the development of agriculture. Fifty percent of the scholarships for the program were for training in the agricultural sector and an additional 30 percent on industrial activity (with emphasis upon food processing, clothing, and shoe production); the remaining 20 percent was divided among tourism (10 percent), infrastructure (5 percent), and services (5 percent). The explicit conception here was to build new human capacities and skills—"Education and Work" were constantly stressed as at the core of the process of endogenous development.

But the formation of new human subjects was not to be achieved simply through skill training. Right from the outset, Vuelvan Caras focused upon preparing people for new productive relations through courses in cooperation and self-management. Attacking the division between those who think and those who do, rejecting wage-labor as such, and emphasizing collective property were all essential parts of this process.

The promise was that those who graduated from Vuelvan Caras and formed cooperatives would receive preferential treatment in obtaining loans and technical support (including means of production like tractors) from the state. All this was in accordance with the sections of the Bolivarian Constitution that called upon the state to promote cooperatives and associations under collective ownership. Development of productive activity under these new relations is exactly what was occurring: whereas only 762 cooperatives existed when Chávez was first elected in 1998, by August 2005 there were almost 84,000 cooperatives with close to one million members.

In short, characteristic of Vuelvan Caras was not simply a program for endogenous development; rather, it always involved a specific combination of endogenous development and the social economy. That concept of the social economy, which figures so prominently in the constitution (with its stress upon self-management, co-management, and cooperatives as the forms permitting the development of people), was not static—it had continued to evolve, moving increasingly from a complement to an *alternative* to the logic of capital.

On his *Alo Presidente* program, September 14, 2003, one devoted to the social economy, President Chávez declared, "the logic of capital is a perverse logic." It doesn't care, he continued, about destroying the rivers and Lake Maracaibo. It doesn't care about denying children an education and putting them to work, about the hunger of workers and about the malnutrition of their children. It is not interested in labor accidents, if workers eat, if they have housing, where they sleep, if they have schools, if when they get sick they have doctors, or if when they are old they have a pension. "No. The logic of capital cares nothing about that, it is diabolical, it is perverse."

Compare that to the social economy. What is its logic? "The social economy bases its logic on the human being, on work, that is to say, on the worker and the worker's family, that is to say, in the human being." That social economy, too, does not focus on economic gain, on exchange values; rather, "The social economy generates mainly use-value." Its purpose is "the construction of the new man, of the new woman, of the new society."

This, then, is the context in which Vuelvan Caras emerged. Its combination of education and work was one that stressed the alternative to the logic of capital, the logic of the social economy which is the logic of human beings. Thus, in Venezuela endogenous development was understood explicitly as human development—true development *from within*. Work and education were a process of developing human capacities and, indeed, best understood as "radical endogenous development," because it goes to the root, which is human beings.

And this radical endogenous development was further understood as involving a radical transformation of the relations of production of the society. With the new relations based upon principles of cooperation, solidarity, protagonistic democracy, and collective property, poverty would be defeated. You cannot end poverty, Chávez regularly repeated, without giving power to the poor.

The growing numbers of Venezuelans functioning in cooperatives indicates that people were responding to the opportunities and incentives that the new program offered. But how much of an alternative to capitalism could this provide? The new cooperatives fostered and nurtured through Vuelvan Caras were destined to be small (certainly at their outset); given their origins, they were not likely to be major sources of accumulation and growth.

Nevertheless, they were a microcosm of an alternative to the logic of capital—one that revealed the heart of the Bolivarian Revolution and demonstrated that the government remained committed to make real the promises of the constitution.

Waiting for Lefty:
The Movement of the Organized Working Class

No one who has observed demonstrations, meetings where Chávez speaks, and organizational activity in the barrios can fail to recognize that the most fervent supporters of the Bolivarian Revolution have been the poor (and, particularly, women). They understood quite early that this was their revolution, and they have been the principal participants in the missions.

The traditional organized working class, on the other hand, was (and thus far continues to be) less of an actor in this revolution. Not only were industrial workers marginalized by the disintegration of Venezuelan manufacturing and suppressed by employer resistance to unionization, but the dominant voice of organized workers in general was the CTV, the trade union federation controlled by the old social democratic party, which opposed the election and government of Chávez. Although there was opposition to the lack of democracy, corruption, and support for neoliberalism of the CTV, it was not until the bosses' lockout of 2002–2003 that this opposition crystallized in the form of a direct break with the CTV's support of the employers. "It's as if the industrial working class had been asleep," commented Nora Castañeda, president of the Women's Development Bank. Now oil workers and workers in several other sectors demonstrated that they had the power to keep their enterprises going. "From this moment the industrial working class in Venezuela began to play an entirely different role."[13]

There was a mood of self-confidence among workers, most evident among the PDVSA workers who boasted that not only had they run the company well, but that they had significantly reduced the cost of production (without all that excess baggage). In workplace after workplace, workers were talking about self-management and co-management, about taking over and running their enterprises as cooperatives. The threat of a capital strike was gone—rather than giving in, workers were prepared to move in.

In April 2003 the process to create a new labor federation began, and that body, the National Union of Workers (UNT), held its first congress at at the beginning of August, bringing together more than 1,300 registered participants representing over 120 unions and 25 regional federations. From this meeting came the clear call for the transformation of "capitalist society into a self-managing society," for a "new model of anti-capitalist and autonomous development that emancipates human beings from class exploitation, oppression, discrimination, and exclusion." There also were specific demands, including "Nationalize the Banks! Take over enterprises that have shut down and run them instead by workers!" and "Create new enterprises under workers' control!"

Taking over enterprises that had shut down was definitely not an abstract demand. Many firms had fatally weakened themselves during the lockout that was supposed to require only a few weeks and then closed down (owing workers substantial backpay). Venepal, a paper manufacturer in Carabobo, for example, had shut its doors a month earlier, in July; the response of workers was to occupy it and to run it under workers' control for 77 days (with the support of local communities and the commander of the local army garrison). Although the workers were calling upon the government to take over the company and transfer it to a worker-cooperative, the company subsequently reopened with the support of cheap credits provided by the government.

But that didn't last. After shutting down in September 2004 and being occupied once again, Venepal became the first private firm to be taken over in the public interest by the government. In January 2005, Venepal became Invepal, a company owned 51 percent by the state and 49 percent by a workers' cooperative. And so began one of the forms of Venezuelan co-management.

Given the constitution's support for co-management and self-management and protagonism in general, as well as Chávez's stress upon the need for new productive relations, it was natural that organized workers would take up the same themes. After all, if protagonism is necessary to develop human capacities and to develop human productive forces, isn't that necessary in industrial firms? If the logic of capital is a perverse logic, isn't it perverse everywhere?

The enthusiasm for worker management was palpable at the Solidarity meetings in April 2004. In addition to discussing the lessons that could be learned from the Yugoslav experience with self-management, the workers' panels considered concrete struggles for workers control in Venezuela. The momentum of workers was clear, especially in the presentation by the "guide committees" of PDVSA, a movement from below based upon the experience of workers in running PDVSA (and distant from the two union leaders who had been appointed to the PDVSA board).

The same enthusiasm and confidence was apparent at the workers' panels in the Solidarity meetings of April 2005, especially now that with the takeover of Venepal Chávez had reiterated that closed or abandoned factories were to be taken over. "I invite the workers' leaders to follow on this path," he said, clearly encouraging similar initiatives in other closed firms. A mood of determination was generated, further, by other experiences as well—the process of co-management which had begun in April 2003 at the state electrical distribution firms (CADAFE and CADELA), where workers' consciousness had been raised in the struggle against privatization and the new example of ALCASA, the state aluminum firm that was to be reorganized on the basis of co-management on the initiative of the government. That combination of experiences pointed to something new being born

The meetings concluded that co-management of production was essential to guarantee and consolidate the Bolivarian Revolution, that it was critical for raising consciousness among workers, and that its aim was to "demolish capitalist property relations and production and replace them with others where labor is privileged over capital." Thus those present called for the government to "continue in its timetable of bringing state companies into this process" and for the process begun with Venepal to continue. "The principle that will guide workers' management and co-management," they concluded, "must be: Power to the workers and the people!" Two weeks later on May Day, workers marched en masse to the chants of "Without co-management, there is no revolution"; indeed, the main slogans for the event, organized by UNT, were "Co-management is revolution" and "Venezuelan workers are building Bolivarian socialism."

Ten months later (at the time of writing), this march appears to have stalled. The guide committees at PDVSA effectively no longer exist, there are significant problems at CADAFE over whether there is to be co-management or a sham, and despite UNT's identification of eight hundred closed companies that should be taken over (and encouragement from government figures that workers should take the initiative), there have been only a few private companies that have gone the route of Venepal (Invepal).

If worker management is an essential condition for the consolidation of the Bolivarian Revolution and the building of socialism for the twenty-first century, then this moment of apparent quiescence is a serious matter of concern. While there are many contributing factors, two problems are likely to be general rather than particular to individuals or Venezuela. On one side, there is a strong belief in some quarters that co-management has no place in "strategic industries." Further, even where this is not an explicit (or admitted) tenet, there is the problem that co-management has a necessary condition: managers who *believe* in co-management (i.e., in the critical importance of workers making decisions). Without resolving this matter (one way or another), there will be no advance of worker management: workers will remain in the position of wage-laborer.

On the other side is the question of worker self-interest as opposed to a focus upon solidarity within society. Not only was the orientation to the collective self-interest of workers in a particular workplace a fatal problem in the case of Yugoslav self-management, but the absence of social solidarity surfaced dramatically in the presentation by the representative of Invepal to the April 2005 Solidarity meetings. We want our cooperative to move from 49 percent of the ownership of the company to 100 percent, he indicated, and further advocated that this be a general course for others to follow. Why? Because cooperatives don't have to pay taxes.

This perspective was clearly rejected by the Venezuelan workers at the April meetings: "Experiences up until now teach us that it is only possible to develop the knowledge of the running of companies by workers when these belong to the state. The workers rejected any idea of turning workers of the co-managed or managed factories into small proprietors." Rather, they insisted, it was the responsibility of workers in co-management "to exert their role as guarantors of the sovereignty of the people established in the constitution, so that the profits of these companies become part of the social funds that help reverse the poverty of wide sections of the Venezuelan population and are not directed toward stimulating new business ventures."

If the level of consciousness of workers in general were at this level, there would be few concerns about the great gap between the life situation of organized workers and the mass of workers who are in the informal sector. However, most of the factory occupations and subsequent demands for takeover have been defensive actions to save jobs; and co-operatives, the favored means. This tendency, plus the stress upon wage demands by organized workers, plus the reversion by PDVSA unions to the old practices of selling access to jobs in the industry, convinced some Chavists that the organized working class was oriented to its particular interests rather than to those of the working class as a whole. Our trade unionists, it was said, are from the Fourth Republic.

The contradiction was obvious: from the side of organized workers, the problem was "bureaucrats"; from the other side, it was a labor aristocracy separated from the mass of the working class. There were signs pointing to a form of resolution of the contradiction, though. In one place, co-management was flourishing: CADELA, the state electrical distribution firm in the Andes. The characteristics were: (1) workers were dedicated to working with and serving the community (a consciousness developed in their struggle against the process of privatization in the pre-Chávez period); and (2) managers, elected by the workers, believed in co-management. But how to get there?

Beyond Capital

How to get to a society in which there is both worker management and a commitment to serve the needs of the working class as a whole? One Chavist who has worried about the tendency in worker management toward self-interest is the president himself. Although Chávez has stated repeatedly that we do not know yet the elements of the future socialism we want to build, there is in fact a consistent and essential characteristic in his conception of socialism—the need for community, solidarity, and socialist morals. "If there are not socialist morals in us," he declared in a talk in Paraguay on June 20, 2005, "socialism is not possible." The values of sharing with one another, of living in a community, of feeling "an invisible thread that unites us to all," of solidarity, of love, and of leaving selfishness behind as well as ambition for wealth ("What a perverse thing that is!")—these are the concepts of socialist morals, socialist ethics.

In this very context, Chávez discussed the demand of organized workers for fair wages and other benefits. They are "entitled to demand them. But the working class is obliged not only to demand its rights, but to constitute itself as a factor to transform society. The working class is called upon to be a fundamental element of social transformation." Workers, in short, must look beyond their own particular needs and consider the needs of society as a whole—and especially those of the poor, the excluded. Isn't it *your* problem, he asked immediately before this statement, when you drive in a car and you pass eight- and ten-year-old children of the street? What society do you live in?

Chávez's emphasis upon the meaning of community wasn't new. Nor was his rejection of both the logic of capital and a focus upon economic gain and exchange values as the bond between people. It was all there in the concept of the social economy, which "bases its logic on the human being, on work, that is to say, on the worker and the worker's family, that is to say, in the human being." All there in the emphasis upon "the construction of the new man, of the new woman, of the new society." What was new was that the concept of the social economy, which permeated Mission Vuelvan Caras, was now identified explicitly with socialism.

What was also new was that Chávez was reading deeply about socialism. Indeed, in that same Paraguay speech, he revealed (as he had on *Alo Presidente* a week earlier) that he was studying Istvan Mészáros's *Beyond Capital* ("a book of thousand and hundred and so many pages") and that Fidel Castro was reading a copy he had sent him. The immediate result would soon be clear. On the *Alo Presidente* program of July 17, Chávez read his nocturnal notes on the book from May 18, two months earlier. There, under the heading "Transition to socialism, heading for socialism," appeared a phrase that triggered Chavez's imagination: "The Point of Archimedes, this expression taken from the wonderful book of Istvan Mészáros, a communal system of production and of consumption—that is what we are creating, we know we are building this. We have to create a communal system of production and consumption, a new system.... Let us remember that Archimedes said: 'You give me an intervention point and I will move the world.' This is the point from which to move the world today."

And what *precisely* was that point? It was Mészáros's criticism of trying to build a new society based upon commodity exchange. The communal society described by Marx in the *Grundrisse*, Mészáros noted, involves not an exchange of things but an exchange of *activities*—activities determined by communal needs and communal purposes. This, Mészáros stressed, was the "Archimedian point" of the system. As long as we produce for the purpose of exchange, the link between us is hidden, and we cannot escape being dominated. To build socialism, we need a radically new type of exchange—an exchange of activities "in which the individuals engage, in accordance with their need as active human beings."[14] This radical reorientation of exchange to one based upon communal needs and communal purposes is the development of real *planning*, not planning from above, but "coordinated societal *self-management*."[15]

The "Archimedian point," the necessity to radically change the concept of exchange, is precisely what Chávez grasped. We have to build "this communal system of production and consumption, to help to create it, from the popular bases, with the participation of the communities, through the community organizations, the cooperatives, self-management, and different ways to create this system." In Chávez's notes, based upon Marx's discussion in the *Grundrisse* (mediated by Mészáros and a translator), we see the focus upon laboring activity which is social from the outset because it is directly and consciously production for the needs of the community, because it is the production of use-values rather than commodities for the purpose of exchange.

But why introduce this abstract theory of a future society on his weekly *Alo Presidente*? Because these notes, written two months earlier, were meant to be made *real*. They were "orientations," guidelines for a new institution, written under the heading, "Plan to create companies of social production, Vuelvan Caras II." Here was a new model, the companies of social production that would incorporate community needs and the community itself into productive activity. A concept that would address the question of group self-interest not only in co-management but also in cooperatives—one which would help to build socialism for the twenty-first century. The development of Empresas de Produccion Social (EPS), companies of social production, along with a complementary institution in which communities identify and organize to satisfy their needs (the communal councils), is meant to mark a new stage in the development of the Bolivarian Revolution.

Reinventing Socialism

"We have to reinvent socialism," Chávez declared in his closing speech at the 2005 World Social Forum in Porto Alegre, Brazil. "It can't be the kind of socialism that we saw in the Soviet Union, but it will emerge as we develop new systems that are built on cooperation, not competition." Capitalism has to be transcended if we are ever going to end the poverty of the majority of the world. "But we cannot resort to state capitalism, which would be the same perversion of the Soviet Union. We must reclaim socialism as a thesis, a project and a path, but a new type of socialism, a humanist one, which puts humans and not machines or the state ahead of everything."

For many people outside Venezuela, this declaration dropped from the sky. However, it was a logical continuation of a path that began with the rejection of imperialism, neoliberalism, and the logic of capital. This very public stance, reinforced by the dramatic defeat of the local ruling class and imperialist coup by a mobilized people and the army, has inspired people around the world with its promise that there really is an alternative to barbarism.

Inside Venezuela, there is also a promise. The gains provided to the poor by the missions have been the most concrete effect of the Bolivarian Revolution. But, it is the ideas of dignity, human development, and protagonistic democracy embodied in the constitution that have enveloped these gains in a vision, that have allowed them to be seen as merely the first steps on a path to a better world. As the result of Chávez's speeches, that new world is seen by more and more Venezuelans as a logical continuation of the rejection of the logic of capital and the embrace of the social economy—a humanist socialism, socialism for the twenty-first century.

Can that promise be made real? The first step in Venezuela was to gain control of the existing state. (Contrary to the beautiful notions of some poets, you cannot change the world without taking power.) And, that state now is being used to create the basis for new productive relations—first by recapturing the de facto ownership of oil (both from the old PDVSA management and also by transforming contracted-out production into joint ventures with transnational firms) and then by using oil revenues to support the development of cooperatives and the expansion of state-owned industry. By degrees, these two ownership forms are expanding relative to private capital (which thus far retains its enclaves—especially in the media, banking, telecommunications, and food processing).

The combination of state industry and cooperatives underlies the new productive model presently envisioned for Venezuela. New state companies in basic industry, telecommunications, and airlines (plus joint ventures with state companies from other countries in areas such as tractor, automobile, railway, satellite, and processed food production) are identified as new forces that will incorporate modern technology and propel economic development. Closely articulated with these state firms and clustered about them as part of new production chains, as suppliers and processors, are the cooperatives, recast as companies of social production. The concept, thus, is one of "walking on two legs"—large companies/small ones; state firms/social production firms; intensive development/extensive development.

These projects are developing new productive forces, creating the basis for moving away from the overwhelming reliance upon oil and generating new jobs for the unemployed and excluded. But is this socialism? Are these socialist relations that are being built? Juridical ownership and productive relations, after all, are not the same thing. As noted in chapter 1, the rupture in property rights, which occurred with the separation of means of production from producers, was a necessary but not sufficient condition for capitalist relations of production; for the latter, it was necessary for capitalists to take possession of production and to direct production to their own goals.

State firms can be state capitalist or socialist in character; and cooperatives can be based upon group collective self-interest or upon the needs of the community. The distinction is one that Chávez has recognized—both in his criticism of state capitalism and in the idea of the development of companies of social production (EPS). After all, there were existing cooperatives, collectively managed by their members, and yet they were seen as lacking. Why? Because commodity exchange (in which they were engaged) implies that buyer and seller are *independent* of each other; in the exchange of *activities*, on the other hand, the focus is upon unity, upon solidarity among members of a society.

In the current discussions (still in considerable flux at the time of this writing) of companies of social production, we can identify two relations: (1) the relation between the EPS and the state firms which form their hub, and (2) the relations between the EPS and communities. In the case of the state firm/EPS nexus, the rejection of commodity relations is the assertion that these productive units are not independent but form parts of a whole, that this is a subset of the collective worker producing specific products in the interest of society as a whole. In the EPS/community link, the focus is upon the creation of a "communal system of production and consumption," the direct articulation of community needs and productive activity.

In both cases, the premise is democratic decision making: the development of relations in which the collective producer is both "the object *and the subject* of power." To the extent that communities collectively identify their needs and set priorities, there is a foundation for productive activity that is truly based upon communal needs and communal purposes. In this context, to the extent that producers in the state firms decide upon their planned activity both among themselves and with the producers in the EPS, their activity is based upon cooperation and solidarity in serving the needs of society. This particular combination of protagonistic democracy in the community and protagonistic democracy in the workplace incorporates solidarity between productive units and society directly into the productive units themselves (the absence of which, we've seen, was a problem in Yugoslavia).

Here is the framework in which people can transform themselves in the course of transforming circumstances. By functioning as subjects of power in both the workplace and the community, people can develop their capabilities and capacities. And, as Marx commented, that development reacts back upon the productive power of labor as itself the greatest productive power. This growth of human productive forces is at the core of "a new type of socialism, a humanist one, which puts humans and not machines or the state ahead of everything."

Which Way the Bolivarian Revolution?

Two institutions that the Bolivarian Revolution has been developing can make this vision real and concrete. On the community level, the creation of communal councils (based on 200–400 families in the urban areas, 20 in the rural) can democratically diagnose community needs and priorities. And, in the workplace, the development of co-management in state firms—a unique Venezuelan concept of co-management which stresses the link between the enterprise and society, where workers operate the enterprises in the interest of the whole society and view themselves as "guarantors of the sovereignty of the people."

The emergence of both these new elements is a *process*—a process of learning and a process of development. Since people develop through their activity, protagonistic democracy in the community and workplace will change them, and, over time, they become the people who understand this particular partnership between workers and society that can build the new society.

But there is opposition to the development of both these limbs of a new socialist society. While co-management advances in ALCASA and

CADELA, elsewhere in management (including within government itself) there are some who do not believe in worker management. To be sure, they would agree to workers being able to participate in making trivial decisions (such as the choice of Christmas decorations, as occurred in CADAFE), but they believe that the important decisions should be in safe hands (theirs).

The same orientation resists development of real decision-making power in the communal councils. Here, however, there is an additional element besides the fear of losing control over economic decisions. Among both existing state officeholders and apparatchiks of the Chavist parties, there is some resistance to a shift downward in power because it reduces the ability to distribute jobs and largess from above (thereby affecting traditional forms of electioneering and corruption).

The economic revolution, in short, has begun in Venezuela but the political revolution (which began dramatically with the new constitution but requires the transformation of the state into one in which power comes from below) and the cultural revolution (which calls for a serious assault on the continuing patterns of corruption and clientalism) lag well behind. Without advances on these other two fronts, the Bolivarian Revolution cannot help but be deformed.

Consider the implications, for example, of the maintenance of hierarchy and power from above in the state firms. The immediate result is the disappointment of workers who believed that the revolution would change things in the workplace (while those who have withheld their commitment have their cynicism and apathy confirmed). The effect is the reinforcement of alienation and, thus, the associated loss to society of existing knowledge and the realization and growth of the potential of those workers—in short, the loss of human productive forces. Without democratic, participatory, and protagonistic production, people *remain* the fragmented, crippled human beings that capitalism produces.

If you say that workers can't be trusted to make the right decisions on matters critical to society, you are saying that you want workers to continue in the adversarial role they play in capitalism: to focus on the struggle for higher wages, on greater benefits and privilege, and on lower and less

intense workdays. You reinforce all the self-oriented tendencies of the old
society and undermine the building of the new. Is the logic the desire to
maximize the surplus in order to devote it to social programs and the
development of new productive forces? Not only do you reduce the surplus by restricting the development of human capabilities and capacities,
but you ensure that workers will demand higher wages for themselves.
The same logic that says there's no place for co-management in strategic
industries would extend to the position that there's no place for workers'
strikes in those sectors. How far away from the "perversion of the Soviet
Union" are we, then?

Nor is the problem of hierarchy within the state firm limited to the firm
itself. The hierarchical relations within those firms cannot help but extend
to the relation between them and the companies of social production. What
kind of democratic discussion can there be between these firms in which
decisions are made at the top and in the collectives? In this relation, the latter are neither independent collectives with the power to make decisions nor
democratic protagonists in a collective whole; rather, they are transformed
into productive units that would have no control over their activity. At what
point would members of the EPS come to see themselves simply as collective wage-laborers?

Similarly, in the absence of a real institution from below that identifies
the needs of the local communities, who will decide upon their needs? Local
officials who reject transparency because of its implications? Local party
cadres? And what about producing for the communities? Rather than the
"coordinated societal *self-management*" Mészáros described, the commitment to the community will be determined by the firms (cooperatives, EPS,
and state firms); demonstration of commitment to the community will
become simply a "tax," a cost of doing business. Is that what is meant by
production for communal needs and purposes?

There is a line from an old Bob Dylan song: "He not busy being born
is busy dying." In the absence of the advance of the Bolivarian Revolution
by the development of protagonistic democracy in the workplace and protagonistic democracy in the community, how different would Venezuela

look from capitalism? All that would be needed is to turn to private capital (domestic and foreign) as a growing source of investment and the Revolution would be back in the position it was at the time of the 2001 National Plan, back when Chávez believed in the "third way."

For some, this would not at all be a tragedy. Should we be surprised if, among Chavist leaders, there are some who want—not "Chavism without Chávez," as often charged, but rather "Chávez without socialism"? There are those for whom development of the capabilities and capacities of the masses is not as compelling as the desire for the accumulation of power and comfort for their families. Everyone knows that there are people wearing the red shirt who are opposed to the revolution. Here is the real threat to the Bolivarian Revolution—it's not the private ownership of banks, media, and other parts of the existing capitalist enclave. *The threat is from within the Bolivarian Revolution itself.*

And this threat to turn the revolution back to the point where it supports capitalism (which is at the same time the basis for a new oligarchy rooted in corruption) points to the need to struggle for the Constitution. To struggle to make real the premise that, just as in the economic sphere—with "self-management, co-management, cooperatives in all forms"—"the participation of the people in forming, carrying out and controlling the management of public affairs is the necessary way of achieving the involvement to ensure their complete development, both individual and collective."

Of course, it would be a struggle to make real Chávez's call for reclaiming "socialism as a thesis, a project and a path, but a new type of socialism, a humanist one, which puts humans and not machines or the state ahead of everything." The struggle to make it real means driving forward the political and cultural revolutions necessary for the economic revolution.

Can that struggle be based upon spontaneity? Or upon sporadic campaigns that evoke the power of the masses yet again to make the revolution within the revolution? Given the enemies of the Bolivarian Revolution (both those outside and inside it), a political instrument that can bring together those fighting for protagonistic democracy in the workplace and in the community is needed. It must be one that can develop and articulate common demands like that of transparency—a necessary condition both for real democracy and for fighting corruption. One based not upon narrow groupings but upon all the popular organizations and representing the interests of the working class as a whole.

How else can the inherent contradictions among those who want the revolution to continue—contradictions between the informal sector and the formal sector, between the exploited and the excluded, between workers and peasants, between cooperatives and state sectors—be resolved except through democratic discussion, persuasion, and education that begins from the desire for unity in struggle? How else can you prevent contradictions among the people from becoming contradictions between the people and the enemy except by the creation of a party for the future of the Revolution (rather than its past)? A party from below that can continue the process of revolutionary democracy that is needed to build this new type of socialism.

There is nothing inevitable about whether the Bolivarian Revolution will succeed in building that new society or whether it will lapse into a new variety of capitalism with populist characteristics. Only struggle will determine this. The responsibility of those who support the process, though, was described well in 1993 by Chávez: "The sovereign people must transform itself into the object *and the subject* of power. This option is not negotiable for revolutionaries."

Beyond Venezuela

The Bolivarian Revolution may not succeed. Not only are there the internal problems that will only be resolved by struggle, but U.S. imperialism and capitalism in general will do everything it can to destroy this revolutionary process because of what it represents.

The Bolivarian Revolution, after all, has put the focus on human needs and human development clearly on the agenda. It has reminded us that socialism is not the goal. Rather, the goal is the full development of human potential. Socialism is the *path* to that goal. The only path.

Capitalism most clearly is not the path. The very logic of capital separates workers from their products, from their communities, from one another. Capitalism by its very nature divides the collective worker, divides the human family—because it must. It must do so if it is to continue to capture the fruits of human cooperation. Precisely because capital's goal is the growth of surplus value, the growth of capital itself, it will never produce the rich human beings that Marx envisioned as the product of a society in which the worker's need for development prevails.

With its vision emphasizing human needs and human development, the Bolivarian Revolution has also put Marxism back on the agenda. But not just any kind of Marxism. Rather, a Marxism that recognizes that Marx's premise in writing *Capital* was his understanding that real wealth is human wealth, human capacities, and capabilities. (Grasp this point and you cannot fail to feel his condemnation in the first sentence of *Capital*—the horror of a society in which wealth appears as an enormous collection of commodities.) Further, that revolution has directed attention to the centrality of practice: Marx's essential point that people transform themselves through their activity, in the course of transforming circumstances.

In this respect, the Bolivarian Revolution has brought back the Marxism of Che Guevara—especially his recognition that it is necessary to act vigorously to *eliminate* the categories of the old society, particularly the lever of material interest, and to build the new human being. What kind of productive relations permit the development of the human beings that can create the new society? Che understood that these could not be alienated relations, that they could not be relations in which the connections of the collective worker were hidden. They had to be transparent relations, relations that build upon solidarity and, in turn, build more solidarity within society. It was necessary, in short, to create new social relations, relations based upon the consciousness of the unity of people (a unity Marx described as based upon recognition of difference).

And Che argued that the development of this new consciousness does more for the development of production than material incentives do. In the discussions of producing for communal needs, of exchanging activities rather than commodities (which begin from the concept of separation), Che's Marxism is embodied in the Bolivarian Revolution—a revolution that has focused upon human development, a revolution of radical needs.

Venezuela has its unique characteristics—oil wealth obviously comes to mind (as does its enormous social debt). But most of what stands out about the Bolivarian Revolution has little specifically to do with Venezuela. The struggle for human development, for radical needs, the centrality of protagonistic democracy (within the workplace and community), the understanding that people are transformed as they struggle for justice and dignity, that democracy is practice, that socialism and protagonistic democracy are one—these are the characteristics of a new humanist socialism, a socialism for the twenty-first century everywhere.

There is an alternative. And it can be struggled for in every country. We can try to build that socialism now. Those struggles will of course face not only local ruling powers but also imperialism. Every place these struggles proceed, though, will make it easier for those who have gone before and those yet to come.

So, today, let us say, "Two, Three, Many Bolivarian Revolutions!"

Notes

1. The Needs of Capital versus the Needs of Human Beings

1. This chapter was initially published in Douglas Dowd, *Understanding Capitalism: Critical Analysis from Karl Marx to Amartya Sen* (London: Pluto Press, July 2002). Reprinted with permission. I am very grateful to Doug Dowd and Sid Shniad for their comments on an earlier draft of this essay. I have taken many but not all of their suggestions.

2. I have chosen to use many direct quotations from Marx in this essay—not to send the reader in search of the source but to convey Marx's point in language more compelling and relevant than mine. Most of the quotations from Marx are drawn from volume 1 of *Capital* (New York: Vintage Books, 1977), the only volume of *Capital* that Marx completed, and from his rich notebooks of 1857–58, which have been published as the *Grundrisse* (New York: Vintage Books, 1973). I have used many of these quotations before (with proper citation) in my *Beyond Capital: Marx's Political Economy of the Working Class*, rev. ed. (London: Palgrave Macmillan, 2003). For some of these arguments and quotations see also my "Marx's Falling Rate of Profit: A Dialectical View," in *Canadian Journal of Economics* (May 1976) and "Analytical Marxism and the Marxian Theory of Crisis," in *Cambridge Journal of Economics* (May 1994).

3. Marx himself did not use the term "sales effort." This was stressed by Paul Baran and Paul M. Sweezy in their *Monopoly Capital* (New York: Monthly Review Press, 1966), and I use the term to underscore the continuity here between the latter work and that of Marx. The importance of "salesmanship" to twentieth-century capitalism was also a theme of Thorstein Veblen.

4. For a good Marxist introduction to the problem of capitalism and the environment, see John Bellamy Foster, *The Vulnerable Planet* (New York: Monthly Review Press, 1999). A more detailed study of the centrality of ecology to Marx's view can be found in *Marx's Ecology* (New York: Monthly Review Press, 2000). See also James O'Connor—both in his *Natural Causes: Essays in Ecological Marxism* (New York: Guilford Press, 1998) and in the journal *Capitalism Nature Socialism*—and Paul Burkett, *Marx and Nature: A Red and Green Perspective* (New York: St. Martin's Press, 1999).

5. Marx, *Capital*, vol. 1, 899. I break here from my pattern of not providing specific citations because, despite its significance, this passage (and others on the page) have not received sufficient attention.

6. Marx, *Capital*, vol. 1, 772.

2. Ideology and Economic Development

1. An earlier version of this essay, "Economics, Ideology and the Possibility of Endogenous Development," was presented at the Sixth International Meeting of Economists on Globalization and Development Problems in Havana, Cuba, February 9-13, 2004.

2. Thorstein Veblen, "Why is Economics Not an Evolutionary Science?" in *The Place of Science in Modern Civilization and Other Essays* (1919) republished as *Veblen on Marx, Race, Science and Economics* (New York: Capricorn, 1969), 73.

3. Adam Smith, *The Wealth of Nations* (New York: Modern Library, 1937), 423.

4. Ronald Meek, *Economics of Physiocracy: Essays and Translations* (Cambridge, Mass.: Harvard University Press), 70.

5. John Kenneth Galbraith, *American Capitalism* (Boston: Houghton Mifflin, 1952), 28.

6. Smith, *The Wealth of Nations*, 638.

7. Michael A. Lebowitz, "Paul M. Sweezy," in Maxine Berg, *Political Economy in the Twentieth Century* (Oxford, Eng.: Philip Allan, 1990).

8. Whether "Fordism" was a conscious model is definitely questionable. Certainly, much of what is claimed for Henry Ford himself in this respect is mythology. For a critical view on the historical question regarding Fordism, see John Bellamy Foster, "The Fetish of Fordism," *Monthly Review* 39, no. 10 (March 1988): 14–33.

9. These examples come from the 1972–75 period when the New Democratic Party (Canada's social democratic party) governed British Columbia, Canada.

10. Michael A. Lebowitz, *Beyond Capital: Marx's Political Economy of the Working Class,* 2nd ed. (New York: Palgrave Macmillan, 2003).

3. The Knowledge of a Better World

1. This essay was originally presented as a talk at the World Encounter of Intellectuals and Artists in Defense of Humanity, in Caracas, Venezuela, December 3, 2004.

2. Wallace Shawn, *The Fever* (New York: Farrar, Straus & Giroux, 1991).

3. Karl Marx, *Grundrisse* (New York: Penguin, 1973), 158.

4. Reclaiming a Socialist Vision

1. An earlier version of this article was presented as a discussion paper in June 2000 as part of the "Rebuilding the Left" project in Canada.

5. Socialism Doesn't Drop from the Sky

1. Adapted from a talk presented to the National Conference of Revolutionary Students for the Construction of Socialism in the Twenty-first Century, Merida, Venezuela, 22 July 2005.

6. Seven Difficult Questions

1. Michael A. Lebowitz, Lecciones de la Autogestion Yugoslavia. Translated by Chesa Boudin. (La Burbuja Editorial, 2005), Caracas, Venezuela.

2. Jose Goricar, *Socialist Thought and Practice* (Belgrade: 1975), 92–93.

3. Carlos Tablada, *Che Guevara: Economics and Politics in the Transition to Socialism* (Sydney: Pathfinder, 1989), 111–12.

7. The Revolution of Radical Needs: Behind the Bolivarian Choice of a Socialist Path

1. Epigraph: Karl Marx, "Contribution to the Critique of Hegel's Philosophy of Law: Introduction" (1844) in Marx and Engels, *Collected Works*, vol. 3 (New

York: International Publishers, 1975), 182–83.

2. Karl Marx, *Capital*, vol. 1, (New York: Vintage Books, 1977), 772.

3. ———, *Grundrisse* (New York: Vintage Books,1973), 325.

4. This chapter is an interpretation of the Bolivarian Revolution. All histories, of course, are. However, I stress this for two reasons. Firstly, in order to free myself from detailing every single source, including documents, meetings in which I've participated, and discussions plus valuable reports and accounts by, among others, Marta Harnecker, Camila Pineiro Harnecker, Gregory Wilpert, Jonah Gindin, Frederico Fuentes, and Jorge Martin. And, secondly, to absolve everyone else from responsibility for any controversial inferences.

5. Fernando Coronil, *The Magical State: Nature, Money and Modernity in Venezuela* (Chicago: University of Chicago Press, 1997), 223, 286, 390, 392.

6. Istvan Mészáros, *Beyond Capital: Toward a Theory of Transition* (New York: Monthly Review Press, 1995), 710–11.

7. Ibid.

8. Osvaldo Sunkel, ed., *Development from Within: Toward a Neostructuralist Approach for Latin America* (Boulder, Colo.: Lynne Rienner Publishers, 1993), 6–7.

9. Ibid., 28.

10. Ibid., 46.

11. Ibid., 394.

12. Michael A. Lebowitz, *Beyond Capital: Marx's Political Economy of the Working Class,* 2nd ed. (New York: Palgrave Macmillan, 2003), 193.

13. Nina Lopez, *Creating a Caring Economy: Nora Castenada and the Women's Development Bank of Venezuela* (London: Crossroads Books, 2006), 38–39.

14. Mészáros, *Beyond Capital.*

Index